W9-BEM-913

10 Essential WRITING LESSONS

A Mentor Teacher Shares Classroom-Tested Strategies and More Than 40 Mini-Lessons That Help Students Become Skillful Writers— and Meet the Common Core State Standards

Megan S. Sloan

■ SCHOLASTIC

New York • Toronto • London • Auckland • Sydney
Mexico City • New Delhi • Hong Kong • Buenos Aires

Dedicated to the Memory of Dr. Bonnie Campbell Hill

Acknowledgments

There are many people I need to thank for supporting me during this process.

First, to all of my students, past and present, who make my job the best job in the world, and to those students who allowed their writing to be shared in this book, I thank you.

I also wish to thank the following:

The staff at Salem Woods Elementary, who first planted the seed for me to write this book.

The staff, students, and community at Cathcart Elementary School. This place has been home for a very long time.

My principal, Casey Bowers, for supporting my professional work, both in and out of the classroom.

Brenda Wolf and Corie Reed—you have shared many ideas with me and have inspired me to be a better writing teacher. Thank you for sharing your ideas, student drafting sheet, and guidance during our biography unit.

Nancy Marshall and Tiffany Wilson, for being wonderful teammates.

Connie Roepke, for asking me about my writing and meeting me for a bite to eat when I needed a break.

Dr. Sam Sebesta, my mentor and friend. I continue to learn so much from you.

Toni Munizza, Letitia Toy, Shelly Hurley, Cynthia Heffernan, Theresa McGrath, Stephanie Campbell, Barb Wagner, and Elsa Uchikawa—thank you for your friendship and support. Elsa—thanks for being my "writing pal." We can go have that drink now!

Nancy Johnson, Katherine Schlick-Noe, Janine King, and Cyndi Giorgis—I have learned much from all of you. You are dear friends and incredible colleagues.

Carrie Ekey—for keeping in touch!

My editor, Joanna Davis-Swing—thank you for your patience, your guidance, and your incredible support. Thank you for asking the hard questions and making me "tell more." You are a wonderful editor!

Virginia Dooley and all of the Scholastic family.

My family—my Dad, my sisters, and brothers, who always ask me, "How's the writing going?" To my husband Frank, who supports me in all I do. My mom, who was still with us during the start of this book— thank you for your enthusiastic interest and support.

Last, I dedicate this book in memory of my dear friend and colleague, Bonnie Campbell Hill. Bonnie, your vision lives on in the thousands of educators you touched. You inspired me and countless others. You are sorely missed. And for always saying, "You should write a book about that"—Bonnie, Lesson 6 is for you!

· · · · · · · · ·

Scholastic grants teachers permission to photocopy the reproducible pages from this book for classroom use. No other part of this publication may be reproduced in whole or in part, or stored in a retrieval system, or transmitted in any form or by any means, electronic, mechanical, photocopying, recording, or otherwise, without permission of the publisher. For information regarding permission, write to Scholastic Inc., 557 Broadway, New York, NY 10012.

Cover Designer: Jorge J. Namerow
Interior photos courtesy of the author.
Editor: Joanna Davis-Swing
Interior Designer: Sarah Morrow

Copyright © 2013 by Megan S. Sloan
All rights reserved. Published by Scholastic Inc.
Printed in the U.S.A.

ISBN: 978-0-545-33458-7

1 2 3 4 5 6 7 8 9 10   40   20 19 18 17 16 15 14 13

Contents

Introduction

The idea for this book was born while I was working with teachers at Salem Woods Elementary School in Monroe, Washington. We were working on writing instruction and a few teachers asked, "Can you write a book that includes the most important lessons we need to teach for our students to become successful writers?"

I went home and thought about it. I began to take notes on the essential skills I felt I needed to teach my students about writing in grades 3–5. Some of these were process things: building stamina to write, discovering topics, elaborating on ideas, learning to revise. Some were also product-oriented: how to write a personal narrative, an opinion piece, a research report.

Enter the Common Core State Standards (CCSS). As a teacher, I feel it is important for me to know the standards that are expected of my students, but I also feel it is important to look to both the experts in the field and to my experience in the classroom for inspiration. As I considered the CCSS, I started with Standard 10: Range of Writing. In this book, I showcase lessons that will help students write over extended periods of time, as well as write for shorter periods. I weave in the importance of teaching students to write for a range of tasks, purposes, and audiences. I also studied the other nine standards and have provided lessons on text types and purposes, including writing informative/explanatory texts, narratives, and opinion/argument pieces. You'll also find lessons in revising, editing, and organizing, as well as specific lessons in writing a research report and a literary essay.

This book is divided into two parts. The first five chapters focus on process: Becoming a Writer, Discovering Writing Topics, Narrowing Topics, Organizing Ideas, and Elaborating on Ideas. Within these lessons, I focus on genres such as personal narrative, memoir, explanatory writing, poetry, and more. The second half of the book focuses on specific text types or genres: Poetry, Literary Essay, Informative Article, Opinion Piece, and Research Report. Within these lessons, there is also an emphasis on process. Students draft, rewrite, revise, and publish. They practice the skills from the first half of the book as well as exploring these text types.

Each chapter topic is divided into several mini-lessons. I am a firm believer in slowly "letting go," so there is a gradual release of responsibility (Pearson & Gallagher, 1983). All of the lessons begin with either modeling or sharing a mentor text, then move to shared writing. Finally students have an opportunity to write independently. During this time, I show how important the one-to-one writing conference is in moving students forward in their writing.

These ten writing lessons are filled with multiple mini-lessons to support the larger lessons. I worked hard to include solid strategies for teaching writing, based on best research and practice as well as the Common Core State Standards. While the first chapters are sequenced in an order that makes sense to me, you may decide to introduce them in a different order, based on your students' needs and the curriculum you teach. The last five chapters focus on text types and purposes, so I would encourage you to teach these when and where they can best support your reading curriculum and other content area units of study. My hope is that you will find these lessons helpful as you guide your students toward success in writing.

 10 Essential Writing Lessons © 2013 by Megan Sloan, Scholastic Teaching Resources

Becoming a Writer: Launching the Writer's Notebook

Some students come to third, fourth, and fifth grades with lots of writing experience. Others come with very little. Students have varied attitudes about writing, some positive, some not so positive. My first order of business is to observe students during writing. I notice the students who, given a blank sheet of paper, start writing right away and those who sit, waiting for a topic to magically appear. I watch students whose ideas pour out of them and those who struggle to write one or two sentences. And I begin to see the students who have a solid command of conventions (spelling, punctuation, and capitalization), and those for whom the use of correct conventions is a real challenge.

I want all of my students to love writing. This is my goal! Realistically, I know they won't all come to me feeling this way; nonetheless, this is how I want them to feel while they are in my classroom—and how I want them to continue to feel when they leave in a year. Someone once said to me, "We have to really sell this idea of writing to a lot of kids. We have to perform like we are competing for an Academy Award. We have to show students how powerful, how purposeful, and how fun writing can be." So that is where I start, introducing the writer's purpose.

✳ Day One: Introducing the Writer's Purpose

I begin this session by asking students to brainstorm all of the writing they do or see others doing on a daily basis. Among the students' responses are texting, emailing, making grocery lists, writing stories, and creating signs. I bring in a few examples of writing I have either written or received over the last couple of days. These include an email, a newspaper, a catalog, and a novel. I introduce each of these types of writing and record them, along with the student-brainstormed list, on a T-chart under *What* (see Figure 1.1). We begin to discuss each idea, one by one. I ask, "Why do people text? What is the purpose of texting?"

Leila answers, "It's a quick way to communicate."

"Give me an example," I prod.

"Well, if you want to know what time to pick someone up, you can text them and you can get your answer real quick." I record Leila's idea under *Why–Purpose*.

When we get to *newspaper*, I ask students, "Why do people read newspapers?"

Jennifer says, "To get information."

I answer, "Right. We get information about current events." I record this on the other side of the T-chart under *Why–Purpose*.

We brainstorm additional ideas to record under *What* and *Why–Purpose*. (See our completed chart in Figure 1.1.)

I want students to see the power of writing. I want them to see that we use writing every day for a variety of purposes. I want students to realize that learning to be a writer will help them achieve their goals. After we set up writer's notebooks (our next session), I will type the list and have it copied for students to glue into their notebooks. This way, students have the list they created as a reminder of *what* and *why* we write.

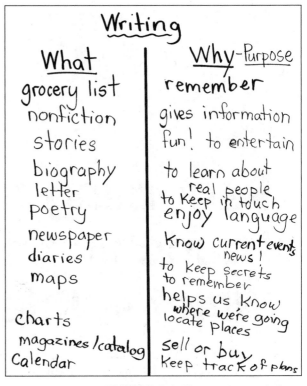

FIGURE 1.1 *Class-generated chart*

✳ Day Two: Introducing the Writer's Notebook

For this next session, I bring in some of my own writer's notebooks I have kept over the years. These are ordinary composition books, some with fancy covers, some very simple. I talk about how I use these notebooks to jot down observations and record quotes I like. I share some poetry I have written and some book outlines. I even share some ideas for a fiction story I want to write some day. I explain to students that the writer's notebook is a very special place, a place to keep your thoughts, record observations, try out writing ideas, draft poetry or other genres, brainstorm lists, and even keep artifacts like baseball tickets.

The writer's notebook is not always a neat place. It is often messy. Not in the sense that the handwriting is messy—but it is a treasure chest of an individual's ideas, and every writer organizes his or her notebook in his or her own way. My writer's notebook has ideas mixed in with other ideas because I write what I observe when I observe it. I record my thinking when I am thinking it.

If you don't keep a writer's notebook, find out which authors do. Visit their websites, go to an authors' conference, read a book, or watch a video of an author talking about the way he or she gathers ideas. The *Meet the Author* series, published by Richard C. Owen, Inc., is a great way to introduce various authors and illustrators and the ways they work to gather ideas. YouTube is another resource for finding out about ways authors and teachers use their writer's notebooks. Don't be afraid to check it out. You will find teachers' ideas for keeping a writer's notebook, as well as authors and writing experts, such as Lucy Calkins and Ralph Fletcher, sharing their ideas.

Sharing a Mentor Text

I share several of the *Meet the Author* series books with students over the next couple of weeks. For example, I always read from *Once Upon a Time* by Eve Bunting. She talks about her attic as the special place she wrote when her children were little. She says, "I write my stories out first in a notebook . . . Pencils are easy to carry, and I can take them any place I go." Bunting says she writes in dentists' waiting rooms, in her car, and in a floating chair in her swimming pool. She carries her notebook everywhere but says, "Sometimes I get an idea when I don't have my notebook with me. What a disaster! But I can usually find something to write on."

Writing Tip

Share your favorite author's processes for writing.

Eve Bunting goes on to explain how she gets her ideas for writing. "Most of my ideas come from interesting things that I've read in newspapers or magazines or books." Bunting shares how real things she read about inspired some of her most famous books, such as *Someday a Tree, The Wall,* and *Smoky Night.*

After hearing about Eve Bunting, my students and I move to other authors in the series (Denise Fleming, Ralph Fletcher, and Janet Wong). We discuss each author's use of a writer's notebook and talk about how writers are inspired by the world around them. I share Janet Wong's book *Before It Wriggles Away* and repeat a quote by her: "Capture your own ideas on paper before they wriggle away."

I ask students, "What do you think that means? Think about what Eve Bunting shared in her book as well."

Joey offers, "It means write it down before you forget."

I respond, "Yes. That is one reason authors keep a writer's notebook." I open Denise Fleming's book *Maker of Things* where she talks about this same idea. "Denise Fleming says, 'When I get an idea, I rush to find a pencil and paper so I can write my idea down before I forget it.'"

Katie adds, "If you have your notebook with you, you can write down anything you see or hear, or a story you are thinking about."

I read from Wong's book again and share her thinking, "Reading other people's books often inspires me to get going and write something new . . . . I do a lot of my writing in bits."

I ask, "What do you think that means? There are two thoughts here."

Jenny answers, "It means she takes her time when she writes. She doesn't try to finish it in one day."

"Yes. I think we need to take our time with our writing, too."

Reece says, "I think she reads other people's books, and they may give her ideas for a next book."

I ask, "Can we do both of those things? Take our time and read a lot so we can be inspired by the books we read?"

Students agree that these are two ways we can become better as writers.

Writer's notebooks

Creating Writer's Notebooks

Once I create an excitement about writer's notebooks, I say to students, "Guess what? You are each going to get a writer's notebook and you are going to make it your own." I hand out regular composition books (before the school year begins, I purchase these three for a dollar). I have lots of colorful paper for students to choose from to create a cover and a back for their notebooks.

Another option is to have students go home and gather pictures of things that are important to them. Pictures of their family, home, pets, hobbies, and favorite foods all work. Students can also cut out pictures from magazines. They glue these pictures to the cover of their notebooks, making a collage of important things in their lives. These pictures can serve as ideas for writing throughout the year.

Once students' books have been transformed from a regular composition book to a writer's notebook, we are ready to begin.

✳ Day Three: Launching the Writer's Notebook— Recording Observations

Now that students have had a chance to hear about how authors use a writer's notebook, it is time to open their own notebooks and begin. I gather students in a circle, asking them to bring their writer's notebooks with them.

I begin, "You know, there is a famous adult author named Stephen King. He writes scary stories and is very good at what he does. I once read that he said something like this, 'People think authors have ideas just drop into their laps. It's not true. We just pay attention to the world around us.' What do you think he means by that?"

Jesse says, "Maybe that authors observe things that happen and then get ideas from those things."

Ryan adds, "I think he means that authors pay attention and when something happens, like the crows stealing the snacks, he writes that down and may put it into a story."

"You are both right. Authors and poets constantly observe the world around them. They use all of their senses. That is where they get a lot of their ideas. Today, you are going to observe the world around you and record what you see, hear, smell, taste, or feel."

I tell students we are going to go on a walk with our notebooks. This is a quiet time for students to observe the world around them. We walk around our campus: by the lunch room, out to the playground where first and second graders are playing, and over to our garden, where a tree and other plants and flowers grow. We walk out to the field where horses stand on the other side of the fence, and a dog barks. Students write as we walk. We stop sometimes so students can sit and "listen" to the world around them and record what they observe.

Finally, we return to our classroom, and I encourage students to share their observations with the group:

- Someone dropping a tray
- The wind blowing
- A little bit of yellow and orange on the trees
- Recess whistle
- Kids playing four square

- A horse leaning down to eat grass
- A dog barking
- Kids yelling and running around in circles
- All the kids running one way at once (after the whistle)
- Leaves rustling in the wind

We talk about students' observations, and I say, "You know, you may use one or more of these ideas in the future. Maybe you want to write about one of the ideas, or maybe you want to use an idea from your list in a fiction story or a poem or something else. Now this list of observations is in your notebook, and you can refer to it from time to time."

Writing Tip

Teach young writers to be observers of their world.

Sharing a Mentor Text and Assigning Homework

One of my favorite poetry books is *All the Small Poems and Fourteen More* by Valerie Worth. I tell students, "I am going to share some poems from this book by Valerie Worth. It is full of short poems about observations: a lawnmower sitting on the grass, a dog lying down to take a nap, daisies growing by the side of a fence."

I read from Worth's book of poems and ask students to imagine that the author is watching something happen and telling us, bit by bit, what she is observing. I continue to read from the book, and we talk about how simple Worth's poems are but how she is able to draw us in to her observations.

"Now, it is your turn," I tell students. "This weekend you will take home your writer's notebook and observe the world around you. What kinds of things will you observe? Maybe it will be an everyday observation. Maybe it will be a surprising observation, or maybe it will be something new, something you have never observed before. Write down what you see, hear, smell, taste, or feel."

I continue, "Watch for things to happen. Maybe you have a cat or a dog. Watch something it does and write it down. Maybe your little brother or sister will do something funny. Maybe you will observe something while on a bike ride, a bus ride, or a walk. Write down your thinking. Make it a poem, if you like, just like Valerie Worth. Come back on Monday, ready to share."

Even though I did not tell students they had to write poems using their observations, many were inspired by Valerie Worth and her "small poems." See some examples in Figure 1.2 on page 10. Students see how poetry is a good fit for writing one's observations.

I let students know that making observations is something we will practice throughout the year. It is a powerful place in which we draw our inspirations for writing.

✳ Day Four: Writing Lists—Modeled and Independent Writing

I love lists. I make them all the time: *Things to Do, Grocery Lists, Places I Want to Travel, Things I Want to Do Before I Die*. I tell students, "Making a list is a great way to brainstorm ideas for writing." I show them some of my lists; see an example in Figure 1.3 on page 10. "I often start poems with lists of words or phrases and then I mix them up at the end to make my poem sound the way I want it to sound."

FIGURE 1.2 *Student observation poems*

Crescent Moon *by Tatum*

Crescent Moon
hanging from the sky on
an invisible hook.
Can I sit upon your swing?
And watch the moon and all
the stars from there?
Please say yes.

My Cat *by Demetry*

White, fluffy.
Blinks her eyes
once, twice.
Takes her paw
and covers her eye.
Jumps to her feet.
Slinks off.

My Feet Saw More Than Me *by Emma*

Sand, water, rocks,
My feet saw more than me.
Sand in my toes,
Water on my socks,
Creatures hidden
Behind the rocks.
They are feeling seaweed
But I am not.
They are seeing sand
Flying up into sock's home,
But it is too soft there,
So it sneakily creeps up
To my toes.
And it's stuck there,
'Till the bath comes.
My feet saw more than me.

FIGURE 1.3 *A sample list I share with students*

Things to Do on a Rainy Day

- Read a good book
- Sit by the fire
- Watch a movie
- Play a board game
- Watch the raindrops on the window
- Tell stories

After sharing several lists I have in my writer's notebook, I tell students I would like them to make two lists for me: *Good Times* and *Bad Times*. I say, "We all have good days and bad days in our lives. Sometimes making a list of these times helps us think of a topic that would be worth writing about." I model in my own notebook first and project it on the whiteboard; see Figure 1.4.

FIGURE 1.4 *My "Good Times/Bad Times" list*

Good Times	Bad Times
• Going to the fair • Getting married • Going back to visit Hawaii • A trip to Ireland • Watching baseball with my dad • My mom • Gymnastics	• Having surgery • My mother dying • Moving away from friends • Hurting my back • Having to stop gymnastics because of an injury • Bailey dying (my sister's dog)

This modeling is important so students can really see what could go on their lists.

Students Write Their Lists

Now it is time for students to do some writing in their notebooks. I give them ten minutes to generate lists of *Good Times* and *Bad Times*. During this time, I encourage students to keep focused on writing. In addition to learning to make lists, students are developing stamina to write for a sustained period of time. After about five minutes, I stop students and invite individuals to share an idea from one of their lists. This sharing serves as inspiration for others. For instance, Jenny shares about her dog dying. That makes Demetry think of his cat getting sick and almost dying. Isobel shares, "Getting stung by a bee." Immediately, Leobardo says, "Oh, my thumbnail coming off." After several students share, we go back to five more minutes of writing. See a sample student list in Figure 1.5.

FIGURE 1.5 *Student list*

> **Writing Tip**
> Pause in the middle of brainstorming for students to share ideas.

Writing From a List—Modeled Writing

Now, I want to show students how their list of ideas can serve as possible topics for their writing. I share my list again and tell students, "My next step is to choose a topic and then brainstorm some words or phrases about this topic."

I choose my sister's dog dying as an idea I can write more about. I place a star next to this topic on my list. Then I begin to make another list just about this idea; see Figure 1.6.

FIGURE 1.6 *My brainstorming*

Bailey Dying

- He was pretty old.
- He was annoying at times.
- They went to the vet to check his hip.
- We didn't expect it.
- My nieces asked if he would be coming back.
- I babysat my nieces while my sister took Bailey to the vet.
- My sister called and said to dress the girls.
- Bailey was being put down.
- We all cried.
- I took the girls home while they put Bailey down.

Students see that I am taking this one idea and telling more about it. After making my list, I say, "Now I need to think about how to write this into a real story about this bad day." I model in front of students. I think aloud, trying out sentences, adding details, crossing out things I don't like, and rearranging ideas. Students watch my process as I work to make my list into a piece of writing. See my first draft in Figure 1.7.

FIGURE 1.7 *My first draft of "A Really Bad Day"*

A Really Bad Day

Bailey was my sister's family dog. He was 12 years old when this day happened. Bailey was a mutt. He was annoying at times, stealing food and barking at things, but when my sister called me that day, I cried.

Bailey was getting old, and my sister was preparing my nieces for the day he would die. This was not going to be for a while, they thought, but better to prepare them anyway. My sister was taking Bailey in for a check-up on his hip. I came over to babysit. My niece Julia asked, "He is coming back, right?"

My sister said, "Oh yes. The vet is just checking on his hip." I was sitting with my nieces when the phone rang. My sister was crying. She asked me to dress the girls. Bailey had a big tumor, and they were going to have to put him down. She would come to take the girls to say good-bye.

I told the girls to get dressed. They asked, "Why?" I knew their mom needed to tell them, so I just avoided the question. When my sister came in she told the girls. We all cried, and I followed them up to the vet's to say good-bye. We went into the room and Bailey was so happy. He wagged his tail. They had given him medicine so he wasn't hurting. The girls hugged him, and we all cried again.

I took the girls home, and my sister and her husband stayed with Bailey while the vet put him down. It was a tough day. This had been my nieces' first dog. It took some time, but eventually sad times turn into good memories. We can smile and laugh when we remember Bailey now.

 10 Essential Writing Lessons © 2013 by Megan Sloan, Scholastic Teaching Resources

✳ Day Five: Writing From a List—Independent Writing

Now I ask students to look over their lists and choose one idea to write about. I encourage them to make a new list about this one idea, just like I did. We review my process from the day before when I wrote about Bailey dying. Students work on their lists as I circulate and confer with those students who need support.

Avery writes from a list.

Writing Tip

Model writing in front of students.

When they have had ample time to make their new lists, I encourage students to tell their stories in writing, turning their lists into stories about good and bad times. They write about everything—from *Stung* (by a bee) to *My First Fish I Ever Caught* from *When Keele Moved* to *Uncle Scott* (see Figure 1.8).

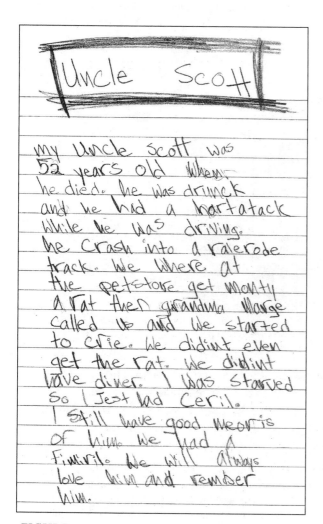

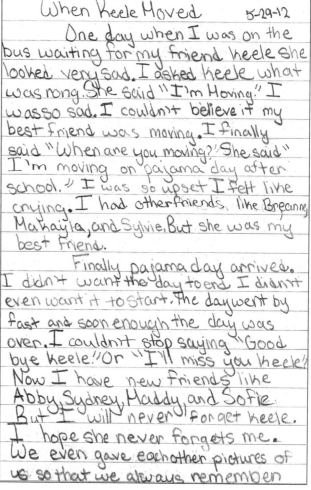

FIGURE 1.8 *Students' writing about good and bad times*

Day Six and Beyond: Letting Real-Life Ideas Inspire Stories

I gather students today to read one of my favorite books, *Miss Rumphius* by Barbara Cooney. We talk about this wonderful character who loves to travel, lives by the sea, and spreads lupine seeds across the land to make the world more beautiful. I remind students of what Stephen King said: "Writers pay attention to the world around them. That is how they get ideas for stories."

After reading this story, students always want to know, "Is this a real story?"

I answer, "I don't know. It could be. Or maybe it isn't." I show a short video of this story that is available online (Gagne & Kerruish, 2000). At the end of the video, the narrator explains that the idea for Barbara Cooney's story came from several places. The character of Miss Rumphius was inspired by three different people. There was a mysterious woman who had come from England and used to spread lupine seeds in the part of Maine where the story took place; Barbara Cooney, herself, loved to travel; and, according to the narrator, a relative of Cooney always said, "You must do something to make the world more beautiful."

Barbara Cooney took these ideas about three different people and used them to create her main character, Miss Rumphius, and the story, too. I offer, "Isn't that a wonderful way to create a character and a story? Barbara Cooney used people in her own life, as well as events and people she read about, and weaved them into a fiction story for us to enjoy."

I urge students to remember this as they collect ideas for writing. "Sometimes our own observations and events we read about can be used in fiction stories that we want to write."

I share some ideas I have written in my own writer's notebook and tell students, "You know, awhile back my dad was in a nursing home for five months after he had a bad injury. I went every day to visit him and I met lots of lovely people. I plan to use this experience in a story I want to write someday about a girl who lives in a small town. Her mother works at a nursing home, and the girl befriends one of the patients in the home." I share some of my notes about the main characters and add, "These characters and some of the events are inspired by the real people I met at this nursing home and also other people and events in my own life. I couldn't have come up with this story if I had not had these real-life experiences."

As students continue to write during the writing workshop, I remind them to take notes about real-life experiences and people that might inspire a story someday. All year, I model how I collect and add concert or movie tickets, programs from plays, quotes I have read, newspaper articles, and so on to my notebook and encourage students to do the same. These will serve as possible "jumping off" places for good stories, nonfiction pieces, or poems. I remind students that Katherine Applegate's novel *The One and Only Ivan*, 2013 Newbery Medal winner, was inspired by a newspaper article the author happened to read. Throughout the year, I periodically remind students to review the ideas in their notebooks and to continue adding notes and observations. The notebook soon becomes an integral part of our workshop.

One day, I notice Avery has been working on a fiction story. She has a list of possible ideas for her character and story. She gives the first chapter a go with a short draft of a lead. She has question marks everywhere, showing that she is still thinking about her ideas. Avery also keeps a page of language ideas. She has written down a simile she is thinking of using sometime, as well as ideas for names for snow; see Figure 1.9 for excerpts from her notebook.

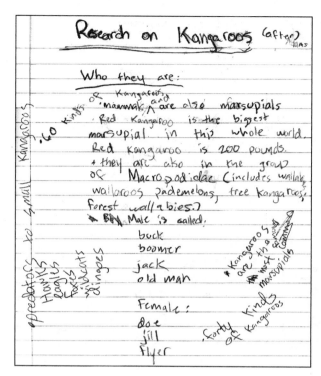

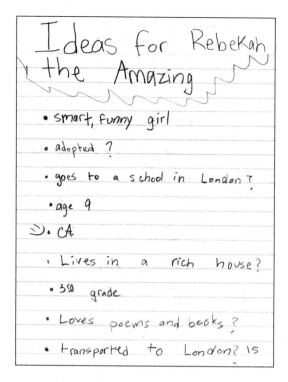

FIGURE 1.9 *Excerpts from Avery's notebook show her thinking like a writer.*

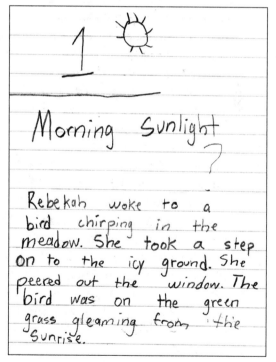

✳ Final Thoughts

Our writer's notebooks are used all year long as students learn about and practice writing various genres. Students begin to own their ideas just like they own their notebooks. Because the notebooks are portable, students can carry them anywhere. They keep students' writing ideas in a safe place until they are ready to use them in a story, poem, or other piece of writing. The writer's notebook launches our year of writing with a sense of excitement and wonder, and provides a crucial starting point for all the writing we will do this year and beyond.

Discovering Writing Topics: Narrative Writing

Teachers often ask students to write about a particular topic. Students might be asked to describe their observations during a science experiment and then add their conclusions. Another time, students could be asked to render opinions about a book or current event and give reasons to support their opinions. Or perhaps students are given a writing prompt such as: *Tell someone who has just moved to your state one of your favorite places to visit here. Explain, giving reasons why this is a favorite place in your state.*

There is no doubt students need to be able to write to specific topics, when asked. But a big part of being a writer includes discovering topics that resonate with an author and will make him or her write with a sense of purpose. Mem Fox lists "choice" among her essential ingredients for teaching writing (1993, p. 36), and Donald Graves includes "choice" as one of his conditions for teaching writing (1994, p. 106). Why? The answer starts with the fact that real writers, those who publish their work, usually have a choice about what they write. This choice helps them write with a sense of passion and purpose. If students write about things they are interested in, they will probably have more to say. Regie Routman says, "Choice within structure leads to high-quality work if the topic is important to students" (2005, p. 177). This structure may come with the requirement of a specific assignment. For instance, students may be working on a particular genre, such as poetry. The assignment is to include metaphor or alliteration in the piece, but the topic of the poem is up to the student. In another case, students are assigned an opinion piece to write. Students decide on the topic and write their own views.

This practice in discovering topics, even within a structured assignment, gives students opportunities to invest themselves in their writing. Then, when they do receive a writing prompt, students have more to draw from and, therefore, are able to write more productively to the prompt. Furthermore, the CCSS do not dictate topic. Instead, they require certain text types and purposes, as well as processes such as revising and editing. Students who are writing a narrative piece will be able to draw on experience, as suggested in the CCSS, if they have a certain amount of choice about the topic. A student who is working on a research paper will sustain interest if there is some choice attached to the writing assignment or project.

✳ Day One: Using Mentor Texts to Discover Author Purpose

Mentor texts are essential for teaching writing. Students need to see how authors tackle the complexities of writing. For instance, if we want students to learn to elaborate on ideas by including anecdotes, we need to show them how this is done by the authors they enjoy. What words do authors use when they include an anecdote? How long should an anecdote be? If we want to inspire students to use interesting language, we need to find authors who model this in the books students read. And if we want to teach students how to choose topics, we need to explore authors who write about topics of their choice and in genres that fit their interests. This is my goal for the day. Because I have a range of readers and writers in my class, I choose a range of authors to highlight. I choose authors based on four criteria:

1. Do I like the authors' books, and do I think the students will like the authors' books?
2. Are students familiar with some of these authors and books?
3. Do these authors write with a sense of purpose and audience? Are their topics relevant to students? Are students interested in these topics?
4. Are these books at varying reading levels that will match the varying levels of students in my class?

I fill several small tubs. This year, each holds books by one of the following authors:

- Jeanette Winter
- Denise Fleming
- Doreen Cronin
- Gail Gibbons
- Patricia Polacco
- Jonathan London
- Douglas Florian
- Gerald McDermott
- Cynthia Rylant

Tubs of books by authors

For older students who are reading chapter books, you can substitute some of the more primary picture books with authors who write early chapter books or novels. Some of these authors include Mary Pope Osborne, Avi, Deborah Wiles, and Dan Gutman.

Of course, any of your favorite books and authors will work. With any luck, students are familiar with some of the books you choose to share. Having read some of these books and/or authors will help students get started with their discussions. They won't have to reread every book in the tub.

Before students begin their small-group discussions about authors, I choose the Gail Gibbons tub and pass out several of the books for students to share with two or three other classmates. Gail Gibbons is a familiar author in our classroom. Students have read some of her books. I ask students to look at the books in front of them and have a short discussion with a friend around this question: *What is the author's purpose for writing this book?* We come back together, and I ask students to share.

Taylor holds up the book *Wolves* and says, "She wants us to learn about wolves."

"Oh, so she is informing us about wolves. Great. What else?"

Jenna says, "Our book *Penguins* is about penguins."

"So what is Gail Gibbons' purpose for writing this?"

Jenna adds, "She is giving information about penguins."

I ask, "Do you think Gibbons is passionate about animals? Do you think this is one of her interests?"

Students say, "Yes."

We continue with our discussion and find that many of Gibbons' books are about animals. But Tyler shares a book called *Recycle*, and John shares one called *Baseball* and another called *Emergency*. I ask, "What else do you think Gibbons is passionate about? What genre does she like to write?"

Aiden answers, "Nonfiction."

"I think you are right. I think Gail Gibbons enjoys writing about true things. She likes to inform her readers."

Jason adds, "She likes teaching kids about all kinds of things."

"Yes, she does. Today, you are going to get a tub of books written by one author. I want you to look at the books. Some of them will be familiar to you because we have read them together as a class or you have read them on your own. Think about the author's purpose for writing each book. Is he or she trying to teach you something, entertain you, make connections, or move you to action?" I also ask students to consider the interests of each author. "What does the author care about? What motivates the author to write the books he or she writes?" I write these questions on a chart for students to refer to.

Now I pass the tubs filled with books to each table of four students. I give groups time to read/skim the books in their tubs. As groups talk about their books, I encourage students to notice any recurring themes and discuss what these patterns tell us about the writer.

After about 10–15 minutes, I invite students from each group to share with the entire class, and we discuss each author's purpose for writing. I collect our ideas in a chart, as shown in Figure 2.1. From this lesson I want students to learn that authors write for a variety of purposes and audiences. They each have unique styles of writing and specific topics of interest. Some write to tell stories. Some write to teach us. And some write to make us laugh. Authors may share common traits with other authors such as humor, adventure, style, format, or genre, just to name a few. However, each author's writing has specific characteristics that define him or her as a writer and separate him or her from other authors.

> **Writing Tip**
> Use books you love to mentor writing.

Author	Purpose
Jeanette Winter	tell stories about real people or events.
Denise Fleming	• persuade us to love nature • give information • tell stories
Patricia Polacco	tell stories about remembered times
Gail Gibbons	to inform us
Doreen Cronin	to tell stories to make us laugh
Jonathan London	to inform to share lovely language

FIGURE 2.1 *Chart of authors and their purposes for writing*

10 Essential Writing Lessons © 2013 by Megan Sloan, Scholastic Teaching Resources

Day Two: Discovering Topics—Modeled and Independent Writing

After our initial discussion exploring author's purpose, we move into thinking about what topics matter to us as writers. I begin by modeling my own process so students can watch how writers contemplate their topics.

Modeling is so very important. Students need to *see* what writers do. Regie Routman notes, "If the teacher doesn't demonstrate choosing her own topic, kids won't understand what choice means. Kids need to see us wrestle with writing choices and then choose the topic we can write about most honestly" (2005, p. 177).

To begin this lesson, I tell students, "I want to think about topics that would be good for me. I notice Denise Fleming likes nature, and most of her books are about nature. I notice Dan Gutman writes about baseball and includes history in his books, so I guess he must know about both of these topics. Doreen Cronin must enjoy humor, because all of her books are funny. And Patricia Polacco—she seems to use her own life as ideas for stories. She must like the real stories of her family."

"I need to ask myself things like: *What are my likes? What do I enjoy? What do I know about?* I really like nature. I like to take long walks and observe little things along the way. I know a lot about baseball and gymnastics. I like spending time with family, especially my nieces, and I used to go camping." As I share my ideas, I begin to make a chart in my writer's notebook. I write the following categories and place my page under the document camera so students can see my ideas.

- My Talents
- What do I like?
- Memories
- What are my experiences?
- What I Know
- People in My Life

> ### Teaching Tip
> Think aloud as you model your process of drafting in front of students.

I then begin to list ideas for writing under each category. For instance, under "What do I know?" I record *gymnastics, baseball, hiking, teaching.* Under "What are my experiences?" I record *taking care of my mom after she was diagnosed with Parkinson's, watching baseball games with my dad, our field trip to Pike Place Market.* Under "Memories" I record, *trying to fit in when I moved to Hawaii as a girl, playing softball, going to the creek by our home in Virginia.* See my complete list in Figure 2.2.

I share my thinking aloud with students, "I notice there are topics on my page that fit under more than one category. For instance, I know a lot about baseball, and it's also something I like, so I might write it under both headings." I do this in front of students. Then I add, "I was good at gymnastics, and I know a lot about it, so that may go under two headings."

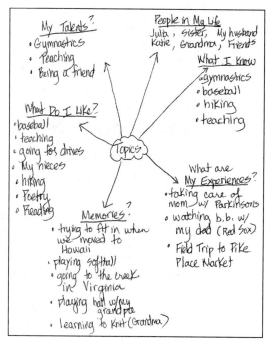

FIGURE 2.2 *My topics page*

Again, I show students how I record my idea under a second heading. I continue, "I think that maybe the categories are a way of determining the form or genre of writing. For example, I may choose to write a procedure piece on how to perform a cartwheel, or I could write a narrative about my experience being a gymnast."

Transitioning to Independent Writing

As I continue to add to my topic lists, I have students think about the topics that matter to them. I ask, "What are the stories you would like to tell? What genres resonate with you?" I invite students to jot down ideas for topics in their notebooks, bearing in mind the kinds of questions I asked myself: *What do I know? What do I like? What are my talents? What are my experiences? What are my memories? Who are the people in my life?* After about ten minutes, I encourage students to share their topic ideas with one or two classmates. There is a buzz around the room as students read topic ideas from their lists and listen to new ideas from others; see Figure 2.3 for one student's list.

Over the next few days, students continue recording topic ideas. I confer with individuals, asking questions and promoting conversations that will help students think of ideas to record in their notebooks. These topic lists will grow as the year continues and will become students' "Power Topics," which they can return to when they are searching for something meaningful to write about.

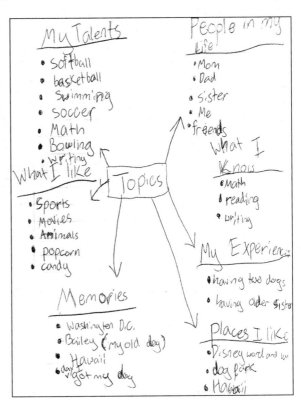

FIGURE 2.3 *Julia's topic list*

✳ Day Three: Drafting a Narrative—Modeled Writing

On the following day, it is time to write about one of the topics from our lists. I open my writer's notebook to my page of topics. I call attention to one idea I recorded under "experiences." I say, "You know my dad loves baseball. One of the ways I spent my time last summer was watching baseball on TV with my dad." I go on to tell my students about my dad and how he passed down his love for baseball to my siblings and me. We watched games on TV, and whenever we could go to a professional game, we did. I have fond memories of those times with my dad. And now, after my mother's death, I renewed this tradition of watching baseball with my dad.

I say to students, "I want to share with you a piece of writing—a narrative story that I wrote last night about this experience with my dad." I proceed to read my piece, showing students my writing under the document camera; see Figure 2.4.

FIGURE 2.4 *First draft of my narrative about my father*

My dad is not a wood worker. He does not hunt or fish. He has no hobbies or special talents to pass along to me. He did not teach me how to fix cars or make things with my hands. However, my dad knows a lot about baseball, and he has a true passion for his beloved Boston Red Sox. This love of the game is what my father passed down to me.

When I was little, we watched whenever the Red Sox played on TV. As we watched, my dad predicted what would happen next, what play would be called, when a pitcher might be pulled, when someone might bunt the ball. There would be yells of, "You bum!" when a player made an error or bad play. And cheers filled with laughter when a Red Sox player hit one over the Green Monster.

Last May my mother died, and I found myself filling my summer days watching baseball with my father once again. Every day we sat and watched. We talked about new players and old players. We cheered as Big Papi hit the leading run, only to watch the bullpen lose the game, again. There were wins too, like when Kevin Youkilis batted in two runs to end the game 3–2 Boston. We celebrated those and hoped for a season where the Red Sox would revisit the World Series.

My father retold stories about watching the Sox when he was a young boy, and I heard new stories too, like the time he saw Satchel Paige pitch against Jimmy Piersall. Piersall got to first base and then taunted Satch, "I'm gonna steal ya," and he did, all around the bases. My dad said it was something to watch Satch pitch.

It ended up being a bad season for our team. Not enough wins to warrant a play-off berth. Disappointing . . . yes. But the time spent with my father, learning a bit more from him about baseball, once again experiencing the love of the game, and sharing a passion for our beloved Red Sox, made it a wonderful time I will always remember.

I read my story a second time and afterwards I ask students, "Do you have any questions or comments about my writing?"

Jesse wonders, "Is this true?"

"Yes. My dad and I really do watch baseball together, and the stories he told me really happened." I point out, "See how the real things in our lives, even simple things, can make good stories for writing."

Ellen says, "I like how you don't tell us it's about loving baseball right away. You talk about other things first, like making things out of wood and hunting."

Ricky adds, "I like how you tell us your dad yells, 'You bum!'"

Johnny asks, "Did your dad really see Satchel Paige play?" (We had read about Satchel Paige earlier in the year, so students were familiar with him.)

"Yes. When he was a boy growing up," I reply.

"What's the *green monster*?" asks Jada.

Domenic answers this one for me. "It's the wall in the outfield where if the ball goes over it, it's a home run. It's green so they call it the Green Monster."

I tell students that one of my goals in this piece was to elaborate on my ideas. (I will introduce this concept in more detail later, but at this point I define *elaboration* as "telling more" or "adding more details.") I tell students, "I didn't want to just list my ideas. I wanted to 'tell more.'" I read my piece a third time, and students help me find places I elaborated.

> **Teaching Tip**
>
> Write about real topics when you model in front of students.

Janine says, "You told about a lot of things your dad didn't teach you before you told what he did teach you."

Jeremy adds, "You told what your dad said when a player messes up, and you told about everyone cheering when the Red Sox did something good. And you told about some of the players on the team and how your dad told you stories about watching games when he was a boy."

"I like your ending," adds Kevin.

"Thank you, Kevin. I tried to write it so my reader would know I was finished."

As students share their reactions and point out places where I elaborated, I highlight some of the lines. I let students know they will be choosing a topic to write during the next class.

✳ Day Four: Drafting a Narrative— Independent Writing

I review our lesson from the previous class. We talk about choosing a topic we feel close to or like, and one we feel we can elaborate upon. I now direct students to their own topic lists. I encourage students to select a topic about which they can write a personal story (a memory, an experience, something they like or know about). We talk about the fact that authors feel a passion for their topics. I encourage students to pick a topic they feel passionate about at this moment. During this time, I confer with students. I begin with Trent. He seems to be having a hard time choosing something to write about.

"Hi Trent. So, what do we have here?" I point to his topic list. "Can you tell me some of the things you wrote down on your list of good topics for you?"

Trent reads from his list. "My family, soccer, my dog." That is the extent of his list.

"Tell me, Trent, which of these three topics is something you really want to write about? Which one do you feel passionate about today? Remember that means you really love it, and it's on your mind right now."

FIGURE 2.5 *Trent's writing about his passion, soccer*

Trent thinks for a moment and says, "Soccer."

"Okay, tell me a little bit about soccer. Why do you love it so much?"

Trent answers, "You get to run around."

"Well, that is really great exercise," I say. "What else can you tell me about soccer?"

Trent continues, "I score goals and learn lots of skills, like passing from my coach and my dad."

"Wow. You have a lot to say. How do you think you would like to start? What opening would tell your reader that you are passionate about soccer?"

Trent answers, "My passion is soccer because I have lots of fun."

"That is a great first sentence. Why don't you begin there and add some of the things you told me about why you like soccer so much? Remember to give examples."

I leave Trent to write and confer with more students. I will return to him later to check on his progress.

Supporting Students' Independent Writing Through Conferring

Conferring with students independently is a huge part of my writing instruction. It is during these one-to-one exchanges that students apply their learning in their own work. I give encouragement, make small suggestions, find an intentional teaching moment, and help students organize their writing. Most of all, I am an audience for a student's work. I must be a listener. A one-to-one conference provides an opportunity to have a real conversation about a student's piece of writing. I am able to listen first, and then point out moments of elaboration, great language, or clarity, as well as proper use of conventions. I also can talk to students honestly about places I am confused or want to hear more. In addition, this is a time when I can ask, "What help do you need from me?" It is important to leave a student's writing on his or her lap, so to speak. Students should be in control of their work. I am here to help, to be a facilitator for excellence, but the students must be in charge of their own writing.

Teaching Tip

Listen to the student during a writing conference.

Student-teacher conference

✳ Final Thoughts

It is important for students to discover their own writing topics. In this chapter, we focused on narrative writing, but we found out that many authors are inspired to write other text types or genres. What is most important is that students learn to write about topics for which they have a purpose and an audience. They need to figure out what topics they have a lot to say about, and which ones allow them to find an authentic voice. What do they already know? What do they want to find out? And what do they think is important? These kinds of topics are the ones that student writers will be willing to draft, revise, and edit, because they will value this writing. It will be close to their hearts.

Narrowing Topics: Personal Narrative/Memoir

As students become comfortable choosing topics for their writing, one of my greatest challenges is helping them keep those topics small. Students tend to pick large topics like "My Vacation" and end up essentially writing a list of the things they did on their vacation. This usually proves to be quite shallow writing. Because the topic is large, no ideas are really developed and, therefore, the piece is boring.

For this reason, I address the idea of narrowing topics early in the year to help students focus their writing. I want them to learn to "zoom in" on the story they want to tell. Narrowing one's topic is tough. Students want to tell everything. That is why modeling is so important. Students need to see other writers working to keep their topic small. They need to watch other writers grapple to include ideas that will extend the topic, while keeping focused. In addition, conferring is key. Teachers need to have one-to-one conversations with students so they can figure out what "stays" and what "goes." Which ideas will enhance this topic and which ideas are just "extra baggage"? Students need help in keeping their topic narrow.

✳ Day One: Using Mentor Texts to Help Define Memoir

Since narrowing topics is the theme of my lesson, I choose a genre in which students will be able to focus on a small moment or time in their lives—memoir. I begin by reading two of my favorite memoirs: *My Ol' Man* by Patricia Polacco and *When I Was Young in the Mountains* by Cynthia Rylant. You'll find a list of the other great memories in the box at right. We discuss these two stories and chart some of their similarities. By doing this, students are reflecting on the characteristics of a memoir. If students can describe the common traits they notice in Rylant's and Polacco's stories, they can work to include these things in their own writing. (This lesson can work for other genres as well.) See our chart comparing the stories in Figure 3.1.

We discuss what makes this genre unique and find an online dictionary that defines memoir as: "A record of events based on personal observation . . . An account of one's personal life and experiences."

Cole observes, "*Memoir* sounds like *memory*."

I agree, "You are right. A lot of memoirs are based on the author's memories."

We also discuss how these authors narrowed their topics. They picked a remembered time in their lives and focused on that. For instance, Polacco wrote about a magical summer. It began as a difficult time, but the belief in a rock changed everything for the whole family. Polacco includes action and dialogue to tell this heartwarming story about a short time in her family's life.

How are these two stories alike?
My Ol' Man and **When I Was Young in the Mountains**

- They are about real people's lives
- They are about families.
- Remembered times or memories.
- About childhood times.
- Focus is on a small period of time.
- Characters are real (or inspired by real)
- You can relate to the stories.
- There's dialogue.
- Simple stories
- You feel the love. in both stories.

FIGURE 3.1 *Student-generated list of similarities between the two stories*

A List of Memoir Picture Books

- *Betty Doll* by Patricia Polacco
- *Big Mama's* by Donald Crews
- *Coat of Many Colors* by Dolly Parton
- *Miss Rumphius* by Barbara Cooney
- *My Great Aunt Arizona* by Gloria Houston
- *My Ol' Man* by Patricia Polacco
- *Owl Moon* by Jane Yolen
- *Saturdays and Teacakes* by Lester Laminack
- *Shortcut* by Donald Crews
- *Thank You, Mr. Falker* by Patricia Polacco
- *The Relatives Came* by Cynthia Rylant
- *Thundercake* by Patricia Polacco
- *Time of Wonder* by Robert McCloskey
- *When I Was Young in the Mountains* by Cynthia Rylant

In *When I Was Young in the Mountains,* Rylant tells of the simple life she and her grandparents experienced while growing up in the mountains. She shares walking through the grass at night, listening to the frogs sing at dusk, and eating corn bread, pinto beans, and fried okra at her grandmother's table. Each author brings the simple things to life through her writing.

✳ Day Two: Prewriting for a Personal Narrative— Modeled and Independent Writing

When I model how to narrow a topic, I deliberately choose one that is too broad. I bombard students with lots of unrelated details so they experience first-hand the importance of narrowing a topic. For example, I gather students and tell them I am going to write about a remembered time while I was growing up. I begin telling them about my grandfather. I tell them he lived in an apartment with my grandma in Bridgeport, Connecticut. He was kind and gentle. He had a wooden leg because he lost his leg during World War II. My grandpa loved to sing Scottish songs and tell jokes. I tell students about visiting my grandparents for two weeks at a time. There was an outside parking lot on the first level of the building. I would bring a rubber kick ball and my grandpa would bring a lawn chair. I would throw that rubber ball up against the concrete wall, and my grandpa would sit in his lawn chair, and we would talk.

I say, "Now, I have a lot of things I could tell you about my grandpa. I want to share a piece of writing that includes all of my ideas."

> My grandfather was special. He lived in Bridgeport, Connecticut. He was very kind. He had a wooden leg. He was Scottish. He sang songs and told jokes. I used to visit him for two weeks at a time. One of my favorite things to do with him was throw a ball up against the wall.

I ask students, "What do you think?"

They overwhelmingly say, "You just listed a lot of ideas but you didn't really tell any details about your ideas."

I invite students, "Tell me what you mean."

Domenic says, "Well, you say he has a wooden leg but you don't tell us anything about that. How did he lose his leg? Was he born that way?"

Sylvie adds, "And you say he was kind but you don't give any examples of what he did that was kind."

I answer, "Oh, I get what you mean. I am trying to write too many different ideas about my grandpa. Maybe I could pick just one or two of these ideas and elaborate on them." I go on to explain that writers sometimes try to include too much. "Their topics are so big that they don't include any really interesting details. It's just a list. Writers work to narrow their focus. In *My Ol' Man*, you'll recall that Patricia Polacco told just about the special time one summer when they found the magic rock. And in *When I Was Young in the Mountains*, Cynthia Rylant focused on the simple times growing up in the mountains. I am going to think of a small memory or time with my grandpa and only write about that time. It could be a memorable experience that only lasted one day, or one hour, or it might be an experience we had over and over during my childhood. I think I will write about the times I played with the ball in my grandpa's parking lot at his apartment. That is a small moment that happened many times when I was young. Each time only lasted about an hour or so, but it meant a lot to me. I am going to write a lot about this little time."

I tell students, "Sometimes it helps to make a plan for your writing. A plan will help you stay focused and keep your topic narrow or small. It will also help you organize what you want to say in an order that makes sense."

I share a page from my writer's notebook with boxes labeled (see Figure 3.2). I begin to plan out my story in front of students. I say, "Okay, first I should write down what happened and where my story took place." (I record my notes.) I continue, "The first event in my story is going down in the elevator and setting up to play ball. The second event is playing ball, talking, singing, and telling jokes with my grandfather. And I remember something my grandpa always asked me. I'll write that down so I remember. And the last part of my story is getting packed up and going back upstairs for dinner." As I share these ideas, I record them in my writer's notebook. The graphic organizer helps me keep my topic small. You'll find a template of this graphic organizer on page 135 in the appendix.

I share with students, "These ideas will help me organize my story, but I certainly will need to add details or elaborate upon these ideas so my story is interesting."

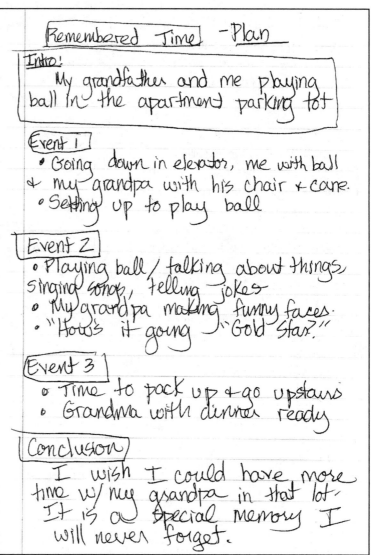

FIGURE 3.2 *My writer's notebook page*

Students Prewrite

Now it is time for students to choose a topic, a remembered time from their own lives that they will write about. I say, "Today you are going to choose a time from your life to explore in writing." I suggest, "Look back at your topic lists and take some time to add to these: What are some remembered or important times in your life? Who was there with you? Was it a relative or a friend? What did you do? What happened that remains special?"

I remind students that these remembered times can be very simple, just like mine. You don't have to go to Disneyland to have a great topic. In fact, Disneyland is probably not narrow enough. So what is "small" enough? I tell students that a "small" remembered time can be a day or even an hour. Maybe, your remembered time is going to the shelter to get your dog. Maybe it is Grandma teaching you how to knit. Maybe it is making your first goal in soccer and the events that lead up to that. It has to be something you remember in detail, a time you can tell a lot about.

Teaching Tip
Helping students organize their ideas will make for improved writing.

Students open their notebooks and work for a few moments to list at least three remembered times. I stop them and invite volunteers to share their times with the rest of the class. This way, students who are having a hard time might be inspired by another student's remembered time. For instance, Alex shared, "My first piano recital." That helped Ryan think of his first wrestling match and Kylie think of her first gymnastics meet. After sharing, we take more time to write down possible topic ideas. I meet with each student quickly, either to help generate ideas or coach students to choose an idea that is not too big. For example, I meet with Tyler who originally wanted to write about going dirt biking last summer. After some conversation, I find out that in one of those races, he had an accident and almost lost his entire big toe. I encourage Tyler to tell about that one time, rather than telling about all of times he raced.

Once students settle on their topics and have met with me for a brief

Name _____

Remembered Time _____

Planning Graphic Organizer: Narrative/Memoir

Introduction: Where/When/Who/What

Event 1

Event 2

Event 3

Conclusion: Why is this story important to you? How does it affect your life now?

10 Essential Writing Lessons © 2013 by Megan Sloan, Scholastic Teaching Resources 135

FIGURE 3.3 *Student graphic organizer; see page 135*

conference, I encourage them to share their chosen ideas with each other. Then they begin to plan their stories using the same graphic organizer I used, and they plan openings that tell where/when/who/what happened. They list ideas for three events, remembering to include their senses and possible dialogue. And then they write a sentence or two in the conclusion section: "Why is this story important to you?"

✳ Day Three: Drafting a Personal Narrative— Modeled and Independent Writing

I review our prewrite exercise from the previous lesson, placing my planning sheet from my writer's notebook under the document camera for students to see. I tell students that I am going to use this plan to guide me as I begin to write about my grandpa and the time we spent in that parking lot bouncing a ball and talking. I follow my plan from my writer's notebook, rereading as I go. I think things over twice. I cross out individual words and whole sentences and revise with better ideas. As I'm doing this, I think aloud so students can see what a writer does as she drafts, revises, and recomposes. All the while, I remind myself and my students that I need to keep my topic narrow. This story is about this one special experience my grandpa and I had together as I was growing up. I share the ways I am "writing a lot" about this little topic. I tell how I feel and what we do when we are there. I include conversation or dialogue;

> **Teaching Tip**
>
> **Checklist of Things to Model While Writing**
>
> - Reread
> - Think things over twice
> - Cross out words or phrases
> - Think aloud
> - Include dialogue
> - Describe
> - Tell how I feel
> - Include an anecdote

I describe the place. I could include an anecdote (a "one time this happened . . ."). These are all ways to elaborate on an idea. See my draft in Figure 3.4.

FIGURE 3.4 *First draft of my memoir about my grandfather*

> My grandfather was one of my favorite people on earth. He and I had many special times together. My grandparents lived in an apartment, and on the first floor there was a parking lot. At one end, there was open air and a concrete cinder block wall.
>
> When I visited, we would go downstairs in the elevator, me with my red rubber ball, and my grandpa with his lawn chair in hand. We walked to the end of the parking lot. My grandpa would set out his chair, lean his cane up against the arm, and we were ready. I threw that ball up against the wall, and it would bounce back to me over and over. My grandpa would ask me about school. "How's it going, Gold Star?" He gave me that nickname when I was in kindergarten because my teacher put so many gold stars at the tops of my papers. I would tell him about my friends and how my favorite subject was writing. We sang Scottish songs together, mostly ones he taught to me. We told new jokes and told old jokes. My grandpa would make me laugh with the funny faces he made. And he would give me advice about life in general. Before we knew it, an hour would have flown by. We packed up the lawn chair and the ball, and we headed back up to the apartment where my grandma was ready with dinner. I will never forget those times in the parking lot with my grandpa.

I reread my writing as I write, working to include more details, listening for sentences that flow, and making changes where I might have left something out or could make a word more interesting. I remind students that there are lots of things I could have included about my grandpa's wooden leg and about dancing with him and the long walks we used to take, but instead I chose one small time with him and elaborated upon that. I narrowed my topic to my time with my grandpa in the parking lot. (Note: I purposely do not add much to my lead or ending because this will be a focus for revision later.)

After I finish, I reread my story aloud to students again. We look over my plan and discuss the ways I used it to organize my writing. Students comment on how I took my ideas from each box in my notebook and elaborated on them, adding more details.

Students Draft

Students now will have a chance to use their story plans from the previous day to write about a remembered time. Before students begin to write, I remind them that our focus is keeping the topic narrow, keeping the topic small, and "writing a lot about a little." I remind them of how I stuck to my time with my grandpa in the parking lot. I encourage students to use their plan as a guide, taking each event and elaborating by telling what happened in detail, how they felt in that moment, who was there, and why this time was memorable. I remind them that they also might want to include what someone said (dialogue), like I did. I refer students back to my piece about my grandpa and me and the conversations we had.

Together, we make a chart to help students with ideas for elaborating; see Figure 3.5.

FIGURE 3.5 *Ways to elaborate*

Tell more by:

- Telling what happened.
- Telling who was there.
- Telling how you felt.
- Telling what someone said.
- Telling why this time was memorable.

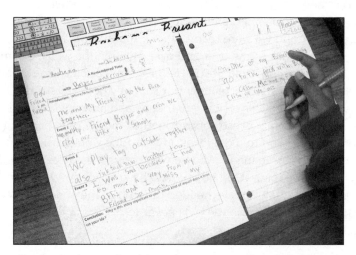

Student's plan and writing about a remembered time

10 Essential Writing Lessons © 2013 by Megan Sloan, Scholastic Teaching Resources

✳ Day Four: Revising for Leads and Endings— Modeled and Independent Writing

I gather students and tell them that we are going to reread our stories today and see if we can improve upon them. I introduce my focus: "One of the important parts of a memoir is the lead and the ending paragraph or sentences." We revisit one of our mentor texts, *My Ol' Man*. We reread the opening page in the book. Polacco begins by reminiscing about her summers in Michigan when she was a child. Her words transport us back in time.

I ask students, "What do you notice about this lead?"

Janelle answers, "It is like she is thinking back."

Todd adds, "She's remembering."

We read the rest of the page and students notice that the author describes the setting (the front porch and neighborhood), introduces us to some characters (the girl telling the story, her brother Richie, and their grandmother), and builds anticipation and excitement about another character, their dad.

I go back to my piece about my grandpa and read my first paragraph aloud to the class. I point out, "I notice that I tell where my story takes place and that my grandpa is one of my favorite people, but I don't really do much thinking back. Let me revise this so it sounds more like what Patricia Polacco did in her story." I begin to revise and come up with the following:

> My grandfather was one of my favorite people on earth. He and I had many special times together, but the one that I remember as the most special might surprise you. It doesn't include any gifts or an expensive vacation. Instead, it includes a ball, a wall, and a lawn chair.

Students agree that my revisions make my piece more interesting and will make my readers want to read my story.

I then move to my ending or conclusion. I reread it aloud.

> I will never forget those times in the parking lot with my grandpa.

I comment, "Well, I did say I wouldn't forget those times, but I really didn't answer the questions on my plan: *Why is this story important to me?* and *How does it affect my life?* Maybe I could add something." I think for a moment and then write:

> I will never forget those times in the parking lot with my grandpa. I miss him dearly. I still wish I could spend an hour throwing a ball up against a wall and listening to all the wise things he had to say.

Teaching Tip

Model your writing after favorite published texts or authors.

I ask students, "What do you think? Is that better?"

They agree that my new ending "tugs at the heart" a little more than my original ending. See my complete revised draft in Figure 3.6 on page 32.

My grandfather was one[1] of my favorite people on Earth. He and I had many special times together. *but the one I remember Most might surprise you.* My grandparents lived in an apartment and on the first floor there was a parking lot. At one end there was open air and a concrete *a* cinder block wall

It doesn't include any gifts or an expensive vacation. Instead, it includes a ball, a wall, and a lawn chair,

When I visited, we would go downstairs in the elevator, me with my red rubber ball, + my grandpa with his lawn chair in hand. We walked to the end of the parking lot. My grandpa

would set out his chair, lean[2] his cane up against the arm and we were ready. I threw that ball up against the wall + it would bounce back to me over and over. My grandpa would ask about school. "How's it going Gold Star?" He gave me that nickname when. I was in kindergarten because my teacher put so many gold stars at the tops of my papers. I would tell him about my friends and how my favorite subject was writing. We sang Scottish songs together, mostly ones

he taught me. We told *new* jokes[3] and told old jokes. My grandpa would make me laugh with the funny faces he made. And he would give me advice about life *in general* Before we knew it, an hour would have flown by. We packed up the *lawn* chair and *the* ball and we headed back up to the apartment where my grandma was ready with dinner. I will never forget those times in the parking lot with my grandpa. I miss him dearly. I still wish I could spend an hour throwing a ball up against *a* wall and listening to *the* wise things he has to say.

FIGURE 3.6 *My "Remembered Time" writing piece with revisions*

Students Revise Leads and Endings

It is now time for students to revise their leads and endings. I ask them to find partners. Each student will read his or her lead sentence and ending to a partner, and together they can work to revise them to sound more like what Patricia Polacco might write. I encourage students to look at their plans to see what the opening lines and conclusions should include. They may also look at my lead and ending for ideas. As I walk around the room, I stop the class occasionally to listen to a student's revised lead or ending. This not only gives positive public feedback for the writer, but serves as inspiration for other students struggling to revise their leads and endings.

10 Essential Writing Lessons © 2013 by Megan Sloan, Scholastic Teaching Resources

Elizabeth
3-22
Writing

A sprinkle added to a special time with my sister!

My sister is a special person in my family. Her name is Abigail Katrina Gojocaru. She is the oldest kid in the family. She is 12 years old. Her hair is brown and her eyes are blue. She is (sometimes) nice and pretty funny too. I think she is a very special person and I will always love her!

One thing that I did with my sister that I thought was special was when my sister and I made chocolate cupcakes! It was so fun! When we were mixing the chocolate. I always stuck my finger in the bowl then liked it. When we were done putting the mixed

up chocolate in the cupcake platters we put them in the oven to bake. When they were done my sister "Abby" took them out. They looked like they were inflated, like a baloon. My sister and I laughed and laughed! But after that the cupcakes cooled off and they didn't look that funny anymore. We started decorating the cupcakes. It was relley fun! There was sprinkles everywere. We laughed and laughed! After that we were all sticky. After we were done decorating there was a mess everywere! Of corse we have to clean up. (That was not the fun part.) After that the cupcakes were all done. We each ate one after we were done with the cleaning. That was one of the special things that my sister and I did. I will always remember all the good times that I spent with my sister "Abby."

FIGURE 3.7 *Elizabeth's final edit before teacher's edit*

✳ Day Five: Editing and Publishing

Students now have a chance to publish their pieces. Before they do, they must work with a partner to edit for conventions such as capital letters, correct punctuation, and spelling. After two partners have looked over their work, either I or a parent helper will finish editing (to ensure there are no grammatical or spelling errors in a published piece). Then students may type or rewrite their stories for public sharing, which could be in a class book of memories, as writing posted on a bulletin board or wall, or shared orally with other students or invited guests. See Elizabeth's final draft in Figure 3.7.

✳ Final Thoughts

In this group of lessons, students learned about choosing topics that are small. Narrowing a topic can be one of the most important decisions a writer makes; it allows the writer to stretch out the details and focus on what is most important. Students who can organize the small steps or events in a narrowed topic can work to elaborate in a way that will bring a piece alive. Students practiced this skill here with memoir. They chose a special time with a relative or friend and worked to zoom in on a small event. With mentor texts and modeled writing to give a kind of "show and tell," students were able to try it out independently with success.

Organizing Ideas: Writing Multiple Paragraphs

PART ONE: WRITING ONE COMPLETE PARAGRAPH

Before introducing students to writing multiple paragraphs, I teach them to construct one focused and clear paragraph that includes an array of details about a chosen topic. I feel strongly that students should leave second grade confident and able to write an extended paragraph, but often they don't. Some students entering third grade need to be taught how to write a solid paragraph; others will benefit from review and practice. A well-written paragraph should include a lead sentence that tells the reader what the paragraph is about, several details that elaborate upon the topic, and a closing sentence that makes the reader feel satisfied the paragraph is at its end. Along the way, we work to include interesting language and appropriate conventions of print.

✳ Day One: Sharing Mentor Texts

Throughout the year, I use mentor texts, sharing paragraphs from familiar books and articles so students can see examples of good writing. I always come back to something Rick Stiggins said in a training I attended years ago. "You know, if you show kids the target, they might just hit it." I choose paragraphs that model a strong lead sentence, several details that stick to the topic and are organized clearly, and an ending sentence that "wraps things up." Some of the paragraphs I choose come from the chapter books or picture books we read, or *Scholastic News* or *Time for Kids* articles. I project individual paragraphs onto the whiteboard, and we analyze what the writer does to make this a clear and focused piece.

One such paragraph comes from Avi's *Poppy*.

> **Teaching Tip**
>
> Teach students to craft one solid paragraph before teaching them to write multiple paragraphs.

With his piercing gaze, Mr. Ocax surveyed the lands he called his own, watching for the comings and goings of the creatures he considered his subjects—and his dinners. He looked at Glitter Creek, home to the fish he found so appetizing; the Tar Road, across which tasty rabbits were known to hop; Jayswood, where meaty chipmunks sometimes skittered before dawn. By swiveling his head he searched the Marsh for a savory frog, then New Field, where, usually, he could count on a delicious vole or two. He looked at Gray House, where Farmer Lamout used to live, then upon the Old Orchard. He even looked, nervously, toward New House. But nowhere did he see a thing to eat. Profoundly annoyed, Mr. Ocax was beginning to think he would have no dinner that night. (pp. 1–2)

As we read and study Avi's paragraph, I begin our discussion with two questions. "What do you notice about this paragraph? What does the author do that fits with what we know about good writing?"

Edgar answers, "The whole paragraph talks about Mr. Ocax."

Janelle adds, "Yeah. It describes all the places he looks for food that night."

I ask, "Does Avi just list the places he looks, like New House, and Gray House, and the Marsh?"

Many hands go up. David answers, "No. He talks about what Mr. Ocax is looking for in each spot, like in the Marsh he searched for a 'savory frog,' and on Tar Road he looked for rabbits hopping."

"He also looked in Glitter Creek for fish. He said they were 'appetizing,'" adds Albina.

I ask, "How does the paragraph begin?"

Angelica reads from the whiteboard. *"With his piercing gaze, Mr. Ocax surveyed the lands he called his own, watching for the comings and goings of the creatures he considered his subjects—and his dinners."*

Trevor gets excited and says, "Oh—all the other sentences are about this first sentence."

I continue, "That is interesting. Avi begins with a lead sentence, and every other sentence in the paragraph is a detail relating to this first sentence (where Mr. Ocax looks, and what he is looking for). Okay, in the middle are a lot of sentences that are details. How does Avi end his paragraph?"

Chase reads for us. *"Profoundly annoyed, Mr. Ocax was beginning to think he would have no dinner that night."*

I ask, "Does that seem like the end of the paragraph?"

Ellen answers, "Yes. It's like we hear all about where he looks for certain creatures to eat that night and in the end he does not get anything. It's a good last sentence."

We chart the ideas from students and leave this up in our room as an anchor chart for writing; see Figure 4.1.

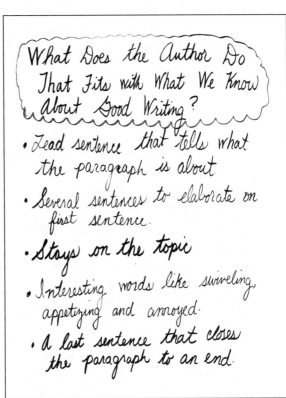

FIGURE 4.1 *Student chart summarizing qualities of good writing found in our mentor text*

✳ Day Two: Prewriting and Drafting a Paragraph— Shared Writing

It is now time to write a focused paragraph together during a shared writing experience. I tell students we are going to construct one well-written paragraph about a chosen topic. "We are going to try to do all of the things Avi did in his paragraph: We will begin with a lead sentence, then elaborate on ideas, adding only details that keep focused on our topic. We will close with a satisfying ending sentence." Students discuss several possible topics and finally choose to write about autumn. First we talk about "the things" of autumn. We make a list:

- pumpkins
- chill in the air
- fall foods
- holidays—Halloween, Thanksgiving

- leaves falling
- football
* school beginning

Now comes the time to write our lead sentence. I have students turn to each other and try out some ideas. I tell them, "Remember, our first sentence has to tell the reader what our paragraph is going to be about."

I ask students for suggestions. Kylie asks, "How about, 'Autumn is a spectacular season.'" Students like Kylie's idea, so I record it on our chart.

I ask, "What should we write first?"

R.J. suggests, "It's not warm anymore. Instead, there is a chill in the air."

"Very nice. Does that sound good?" I ask the rest of the class. Students are in agreement, and I record R.J.'s idea. Then I ask, "What else could we say about the cool air? Does this change the way we dress?"

Albina adds, "We start to wear sweaters and scarves to keep the wind away from our skin."

Ellen says, "And we drink hot drinks to keep us warm."

"Like what?" I prod.

"Like cider and hot cocoa," she adds.

"Hot cocoa with marshmallows," Domenic says.

"Okay. This is sounding great." I continue to write. "How about what fall looks like? Can we say anything about that?"

"The colors of the world change in autumn," Kelton suggests.

Angelica adds, "Red, yellow, and orange leaves twirl in the air and dance to the ground."

Domenic says, "Pumpkins pop up in fields, and sunflowers grow tall."

I praise students for their ideas and continue to encourage them to extend their thinking. "What else makes autumn spectacular?"

Elizabeth answers, "Halloween comes, and everyone dresses up in costumes. Kids carve pumpkins, and everyone gets candy."

At this point, Keven suggests, "We should say, 'some scary and some funny' about the pumpkins." We revise this sentence and end up with: *Kids carve pumpkins, some scary and some funny, and everyone gets candy.*

Cole wants to add something about football. He suggests, "Football is in the air. We cheer for the Huskies and the Seahawks and hope they will win."

I suggest we reread our paragraph to see if it makes sense and is complete. Then we can see if we are ready for an ending sentence. After reading our piece, Kelton says, "We should end with 'Soon it will be winter, but for now we enjoy the awesomeness of autumn.'" See Figure 4.2 for our complete paragraph.

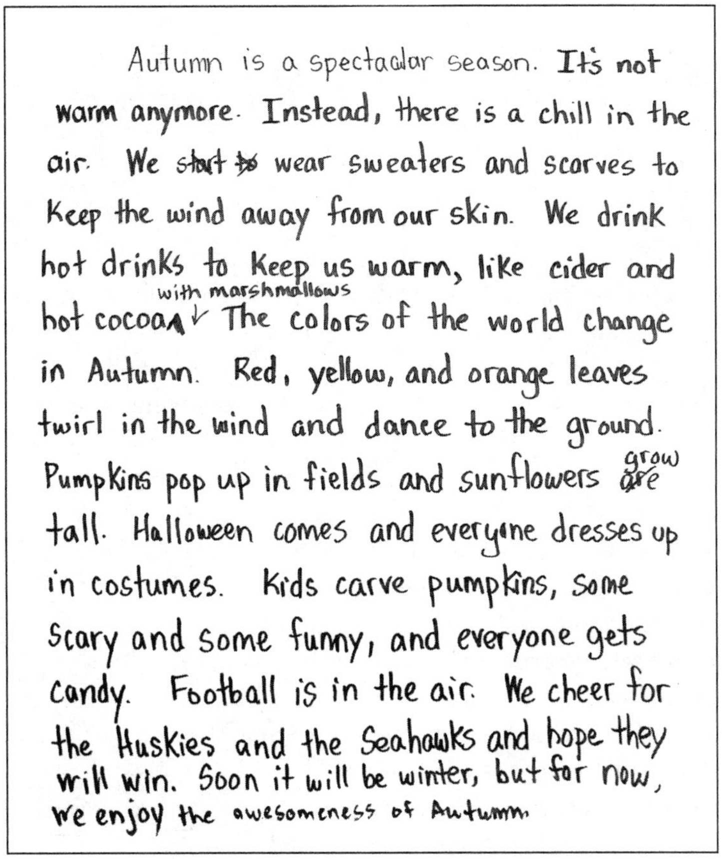

> Autumn is a spectacular season. It's not warm anymore. Instead, there is a chill in the air. We start to wear sweaters and scarves to keep the wind away from our skin. We drink hot drinks to keep us warm, like cider and hot cocoa with marshmallows. The colors of the world change in Autumn. Red, yellow, and orange leaves twirl in the wind and dance to the ground. Pumpkins pop up in fields and sunflowers grow tall. Halloween comes and everyone dresses up in costumes. Kids carve pumpkins, some scary and some funny, and everyone gets candy. Football is in the air. We cheer for the Huskies and the Seahawks and hope they will win. Soon it will be winter, but for now, we enjoy the awesomeness of Autumn.

FIGURE 4.2. *Student shared writing about autumn*

Students are happy with our paragraph. We reread it and identify all of the details we included. It stays posted on a chart in our room as an example of a well written paragraph. We will use it as a mentor text for future writing.

✳ Day Three: Prewriting and Drafting a Paragraph—Independent Writing

Now it is time for students to try this out on their own, with some guidance from me. To make this task easier, I invite students to choose one of the other seasons: winter, spring, or summer. In their writer's notebooks, students write down as many ideas about one season as they can think of. For instance, if I were writing about spring, I might list:

- blooming flowers
- warm breeze
- tulips popping up
- light jackets

- a time of rebirth
- green coming back on the trees
- cherry blossoms
- baseball

I model a partial list so students can see how I do it. Now it is their turn. As students begin to jot down ideas, I roam the room, helping those who need encouragement and ideas.

A Conference With Ethan

Ethan is stuck. He cannot decide between winter and summer. I suggest he make a T-chart. On one side he can list *winter*, and on the other side he will list *summer*. I show Ethan how to do this. Then I say, "Let's see if we can come up with ideas for both, and then you can see which list is more interesting to write about."

Ethan begins with winter. He writes *snow, sledding, Christmas,* and a few more ideas. I encourage him, "That's a great start. What else can you say about winter?"

Ethan says, "Hot chocolate."

"Great!" I say. "Write that down. What else do you think about when you think of winter?"

Ethan answers, "Sitting by the fire." He writes this down. Then says, "Oh." He writes *books* and explains, "I read a lot during winter." Ethan continues with winter ideas and then shifts to *summer*. He writes things like *camp, ice cream, the beach, Fourth of July.*

When Ethan seems to be at a stopping point, I ask if he has decided which season he would like to write about: summer or winter. Ethan chooses winter. I remind him that he may want to write about summer sometime in the future. He already has a great prewrite list ready; see his list in Figure 4.3.

As I see students are midway through this task, I encourage them to share their lists. We shout out ideas for different seasons, and I invite students to borrow from their classmates. "If you hear an idea you would like to write on your list, go ahead. Writers borrow ideas from each other all the time."

Reviewing Elements of a Good Paragraph

After students have made their lists, I direct them back to our shared paragraph about autumn. We talk about the elements of a good paragraph:

- *A lead sentence.* I tell students this sentence should include the name of the season they are writing about. For example: *Spring is one of my favorite seasons* or *The most magical time of year is springtime.*

> **Teaching Tip**
>
> T-charts can help writers sort their ideas.

Winter	Summer
snow	camp
sledding	fire
Chrismas	family
family	swimming
preasents	sports
snowmans	books
snowball fight	walks
feasts	ice cream
hot choclate	animals
fire	friends
books	beach
animals	nabrhood
friends	vacations
nabrhood	boy scout
boy scout	parteys
parteys	Hot July
new year	Starting school
Thacksgiving	stores
	fishing

FIGURE 4.3 *Ethan's Winter/Summer T-chart*

 10 Essential Writing Lessons © 2013 by Megan Sloan, Scholastic Teaching Resources

- *Several details*, which they will get from their list. I remind students that they cannot just list ideas; they must take each one and elaborate. For instance, if I want to include "cherry blossoms," I must put this idea into one or more sentences, like: *The cherry blossoms are everywhere. I love the pale pink trees best. They smell delightful, and their beauty makes me smile. When the petals begin to fall, they cover the ground, looking like a spring snow.*

- *Interesting words.* I invite students to challenge themselves and include some words that are out of the ordinary. We talk about words all the time when we read and write.

- *An ending sentence* that tells your reader your paragraph is finished. This sentence should also have the name of the season you are writing about. For instance: *Spring makes me happy.* or *I just love spring.*

Students begin to work on their writing. I encourage students to hold off on choosing their title. They might want to have a "working title" which might be just the name of the season. Later on, they can change it, if they like, building on the name of the season.

Small-Group Lesson

I look for any students who might be having a hard time getting started. I notice three students who have their list ready but seem to be reluctant in writing a lead sentence. I gather Albina, Frank, and Kevin. I also make an announcement, inviting any other students who need some ideas for a lead sentence to join us. We work up by the whiteboard and brainstorm some possible lead sentences. I start by sharing, "How about *[Season] is a wonderful time of year.*" I write this on the board. "What else would work? Remember, the name of your season has to be in the sentence."

> **Teaching Tip**
>
> Pull together writers who are having trouble starting for a quick mini-lesson.

Kevin shares, *"I just love [season]."* I record Kevin's idea on the board.

Albina adds, *"[Season] is the best time of the year!"* I add this to the two other ideas.

I tell students, "You may use one of these ideas or you may use a different idea for your lead sentence." Students talk it over and make a decision about their lead sentence. Then they go off to begin writing.

I stick with Albina and make sure she gets her first sentence down. Then I help her add her next sentence using ideas from her notebook.

"I see you are writing about summer."

Albina answers, "Yes. I like summer a lot."

"Oh good. You will probably have a lot to say then. I see you have your first sentence: *Summer is the best time of the year.* That's a great start. Let's look at your list. Why is summer the best time of the year?"

"It is warm, and you get to go swimming."

"Wonderful. I see you put swimming down on your idea list. Would you like to add the sentence you just told me?" Albina writes her idea. Then I suggest, "Maybe you can elaborate on that thought. Tell me more about swimming."

"Well, we go to the lake by our house. My mom packs a picnic, and my little sister and I get to swim while my mom watches us."

"That sounds like a wonderful time. I love what you just said. You must write that down before you forget. Now, say it again for me."

Albina repeats her thought and then writes it down. We talk for a bit longer about swimming, and it seems Albina is off to a good start. I encourage her to focus on just a few ideas from her list (she puts a star by them) and tell a lot about each of them; see her paragraph in Figure 4.4.

FIGURE 4.4 *Albina's writing about summer*

Summer

Summer is the best time of year. It's warm and you get to go swimming. We go to the lake by my house. My mom packs a lunch and my little sister and I get to swim while my mom watches us. We float on our backs and play in the sand. My sister likes to build little sand castles. She gets pretty sandy but so do I. When we get hungry we sit on our towels and eat sandwiches and chips. Then we go back in the water. I love it best when it is really hot out. The water cools you off. You cannot swim in fall or winter or spring. That is why I like summer best.

PART TWO: WRITING MULTIPLE PARAGRAPHS

I am now beginning to notice students' progress in writing one complete paragraph. With reminders, they are using lead sentences. They are also elaborating on ideas with several details and ending with sentences that close the topic. Overall, their paragraphs are more focused. As students become competent in writing one solid paragraph, it is time to teach them to expand and organize ideas into multiple paragraphs.

✳ Day One: Drafting Multiple Paragraphs—Shared Writing

If you prefer, the previous lesson can be tweaked to teach students to write several paragraphs. A favorite season is a great topic for introducing multi-paragraph writing. The beginning of the lesson is the same. We brainstorm "autumn things." When we begin to write, instead of including lots of different ideas into one paragraph, we choose one idea about autumn from our chart as the focus for each paragraph.

For instance, students decide to write two paragraphs. They choose to focus the first paragraph on the weather and the colors of autumn. The second paragraph focuses on the holidays in autumn. As teacher, I guide students and keep them focused as we write each paragraph.

This is a natural time to introduce transition sentences. Try to steer students away from sentences like *The second thing I like about autumn is . . .* or *Second, let me tell you . . .* These kinds of transitional words can make a piece very boring and don't help students score well on assessments either. Instead, try to show students in your own writing (and in shared writing) more natural ways to transition. For instance,

> **Teaching Tip**
>
> Take time to teach about transition words or phrases to connect paragraphs.

just using the topic (in this case, the word *autumn*) in the lead sentence of the second paragraph can connect the two paragraphs together, and will serve as a smooth transition.

Figure 4.5 shows an example of our shared writing of two paragraphs about autumn. Again, we decide on a lead sentence. Then, we remind ourselves that everything in the first paragraph should be about the weather and the colors of autumn. When we get to the second paragraph, we focus on holidays in autumn. (Following the same structure, this lesson could easily be adapted to teach students to write three or four paragraphs about autumn.)

FIGURE 4.5 *Shared writing about autumn*

Autumn is an amazing season. There is so much to experience. The weather begins to change as the air gets cooler. Look around and see the beautiful colors. Yellow leaves dance in the wind. Reds and oranges flutter around you before they drift toward the ground. Kids jump into nature's multi-colored cushions, and adults try to rake and bag the leaves before the wind comes and sweeps them through the air again.

There are some great holidays in autumn. One is Halloween. Pumpkins begin to show up everywhere: in fields, on porches, and even on kitchen tables as they are being gutted and carved. Children dress up in their favorite disguises and try to fool their neighbors into giving them candy (which is pretty easy since that is the reason for this holiday). Some kids go to parties and bob for apples or play games. Thanksgiving is also an autumn holiday. This is the one time we eat until our bellies bust. Cornbread, turkey, stuffing, and pumpkin pie are everyone's favorites. Relatives come together to give thanks for all they have. Autumn is truly a wonderful season.

As we reread our piece, we count the details included in each paragraph.

✳ Day Two: Drafting Multiple Paragraphs—Shared-to-Independent Writing

When choosing a topic for a shared-to-independent writing piece, take stock of where you are in the year. What is relevant right now for your students? What are they excited about? What shared experiences are they having? For instance, are students talking a lot about specific sports they are playing or watching? Have you had conversations about pets lately? Have you just experienced a field trip together? Are you studying about a particular topic in science or social studies (weather, landforms, different cultures)? Have students just read an interesting article in *Scholastic News*? Has it just begun to snow for the first time this season? Choosing a relevant topic, one that students have a lot to contribute to, will

Teaching Tip

For shared writing, guide students toward topics that are relevant—ones that foster excitement from students, ones that are in the "here and now."

make the shared writing experience more meaningful, and therefore students will come away from this time having learned a lot about writing.

It is December, and all that is magical about this month fills the air. Students are talking about decorating their trees, celebrating Hanukkah, baking with relatives, and the possibility of snow. They are excited, and when this happens, I realize we have a great writing topic right in front of us. Since we are going to work together on part of this piece, we have to agree on a topic. Students agree to write about December.

We are working on writing a multi-paragraph piece. We begin by brainstorming all of the "things" we think of when we think of December. These include sights, sounds, tastes, smells, and feelings.

Now I tell students we are going to do some planning for our multi-paragraph piece. I think aloud as I repeat several

FIGURE 4.6 *Chart of student-generated ideas for December*

things I see written on our chart: *snow, Christmas, Hanukkah, decorations, Santa, family, reindeer,* and more. I tell students that I would like to begin our piece with a short paragraph introducing December.

I ask students for help as we construct our first paragraph.

> December is one of our favorite months. It is filled with so many fabulous sights and sounds. Winter begins this month. There is a bustle in the streets and in the air. Everyone seems to be in a good mood.

Now I look to our chart. I tell students, "We have so many great ideas on our chart about December. We need to decide on one of them for our next paragraph. Once we pick our topic, we need to stick to it."

Taylor suggests, "How about snow?"

Students agree, and we begin to write paragraph two. I tell students, "Remember, everything in this paragraph has to be connected to snow." As I write, students contribute ideas. We stop and reread several times as we go, making changes and fixing mistakes.

> Sometimes it snows in December. When it does, it is absolutely wondrous. Tiny flakes float down like ivory feathers. They make a beautiful white blanket that covers the earth. Tree branches are clothed with alabaster sweaters. Kids make a snowman, gathering scarves and carrots and raisins to decorate his face and body. Snowball fights appear and some children lie down in the cold to make angels on the ground.

We are finished, so we reread our paragraph one more time. We agree our focus was snow throughout. Now I ask students, "Let's go back to our chart. What should our next paragraph be about?" Students make suggestions and settle on "Santa." We talk about ideas, and I remind students that everything in our next paragraph will be about Santa. We go through the same process we did writing our paragraph about snow. Students share ideas and elaborate upon each one. I guide students with questions. As we finish our thinking, I remind students that we want to end with a short closing paragraph that leaves our reader satisfied. I explain to students that one way to do this is by having our ending sentences include the main topic word (in this case, *December*). The closing should also give the reader the feeling that the piece is finished. The reader should not be turning the page wondering if there is more.

Teaching Tip

For the closing paragraph, teach students to include the main topic word from the piece and craft sentences that leave the reader satisfied. Sometimes the closing paragraph restates the introductory paragraph, using different words.

Our third paragraph reads:

Santa is a big part of December. He brings gifts to good kids who have been "nice" all year long. Many families take pictures with Santa at the malls. The little babies sit on his lap. Young boys and girls tell him what they wish for. Then, on Christmas Eve, Santa sneaks down the chimney and fills stockings that have been hung "with care."

Our closing paragraph reads:

December is truly a magical month. We look forward to it all year, and before you know it, it's over and we have eleven more months until next December.

✳ Day Three: Drafting Multiple Paragraphs— Independent Writing

Now it is time for students to write a multi-paragraph piece about December on their own. They use our "December Things" chart to inspire their thinking, choosing one focus for each paragraph. I encourage students to write down ideas in their notebooks for each of their paragraphs. As they begin to write, remind students to introduce the month with a lead sentence or paragraph. At the end of their piece, they are to write an ending sentence. I also encourage students to include interesting and specific language to describe December. See Avery's complete piece in Figure 4.7 on page 44.

After students write their draft, I ask them to assess their writing using a checklist to help with any needed revising or editing. This checklist asks students to evaluate whether they have included the key elements of writing we have been working on: lead sentences, elaboration of ideas, the use of interesting words, inclusion of capitals and periods, and an ending sentence. It also asks students to identify the focus of each paragraph. By completing this checklist, students really need to reflect thoughtfully on their writing. See Avery's assessment checklist in Figure 4.8 on page 44; you'll find a template of this form on page 136.

Avery
12-10
Writing

December Glory

December is a great month! Snow piles up in my yard. We can make dazzling snowangels, sprakling snowmen and icy snowballs. The snowmen seem to wave with the wind rushing across my face.

In December the food is delicovis! Candy canes, oranges, roast beef, and cookies are great treats! Every year we go and eat food at my grandparent's house and feast and feast on glorious food.

Every year a speacil holiday is around the corner... Christmas! We go to are grandparent's house and act out the Nativity play. We get presents from Santa and are parents too. We also get are christmas tree for the presents to go under.

In December the decorations are splendid! Lights seem to wink and talk to you. Ornaments hang from are wonderful tree! And wreaths dangle at my door. Every year people down are street hang up amazing christmas lights! When we are out late at night, we go past are house to go look at the reds, greens, whites, yellows, and blues. In December happiness spreads!

FIGURE 4.7 *Avery's piece of writing*

Name Avery _____   ④ Exceeded Date 12-10
the standard

Wonderful piece of writing!
You have great details!

DECEMBER WRITING

	Yes	No
1. I have a title.	V	__
2. I have a lead sentence.	V	__
3. I elaborated with details.	V	__
4. I used interesting words.	V	__

They are *dazzling*★
glourious★   Your word choices are splendid!

| 5. I have an ending sentence. | V |

★ 6. I have at least two paragraphs with two main ideas. My first paragraph is about ___snow___. My second paragraph is about ___food___.

★ I indented my paragraphs and checked for spelling and capital letters. V

Beautiful!

FIGURE 4.8 *Avery's assessment of her writing*

✳ Final Thoughts

Learning to write more than one paragraph on a topic can seem a bit overwhelming at first. Starting with how to write one solid paragraph by dissecting model paragraphs in the books and articles students read is a great way to start. Then students are ready to tackle writing a solid paragraph themselves. Once they have accomplished that task, students will be ready to write multiple paragraphs. What is important here is to choose topics that will allow students to break apart the details into several paragraphs. Students have to feel they have enough details to share in each paragraph. Doing lots of modeled and shared writing first will support students when they are ready to try independently.

Elaborating on Ideas: A Close Look at Telling More

As a young writer, I was taught to add details to my stories, essays, and research papers. I knew this was important because details made my writing longer, and longer was always a good thing, or so I thought. But I was a bit confused about what it meant to add details. I was never given any strategies for this.

When I began teaching I knew I needed to instruct my students to add details to their writing, not for length, but because details are what makes a piece rich. I also knew I needed to teach students *how* to do this. I realized I would need to break this down a bit, and show students specific ways to elaborate. So I began to look at what writers do when they elaborate in their stories and other texts.

ELABORATING BY "TELLING MORE"

While I have encouraged students to "tell more" in previous lessons, I have not gone into too much detail about specific techniques for doing this. Therefore, I decide to focus my next big lesson on elaborating on ideas so I can specifically introduce students to some of the strategies for "telling more." As always, I begin with the books in my classroom.

✳ Day One: Sharing a Mentor Text to Define Elaboration

I introduce this lesson by sharing a paragraph from a former read-aloud, *Because of Winn-Dixie* by Kate DiCamillo. I set the scene: "This is the part near the beginning of the story, after Opal has found the dog, and she is trying to clean him up before showing him to the preacher."

When I was done working on him, Winn-Dixie looked a whole lot better. He still had his bald spots, but the fur that he did have cleaned up nice. It was all shiny and soft. You could still see his ribs, but I intended to feed him good and that would take care of that. I couldn't do anything about his crooked yellow teeth because he got into a sneezing fit every time I started brushing them with my toothbrush, and I finally had to give up. But for the most part, he looked a whole lot better, and so I took him into the trailer and showed him to the preacher.

I project this paragraph onto the board as I read it aloud to students. We discuss the merits of the writing. There is a lead sentence. There are some details, and the paragraph's last sentence lets us know the paragraph is at its end, projecting us into the next scene.

I ask students, "What is this paragraph about?"

Jayger answers, "Opal is trying to clean up Winn-Dixie before she takes him to see the preacher."

"That's right. In the first sentence, Opal states, 'When I was done working on him, Winn-Dixie looked a whole lot better.' What does Opal tell us in the sentences that follow?"

Domenic answers, "She tells us that he still has bald spots but the fur he has looks cleaner."

Ryan adds, "And she says his fur is shiny and soft but you could still see his ribs."

I add, "Yes. Does she have a plan for that?"

Isabella answers, "She's going to feed him good."

Jaden adds, "And then she says she couldn't fix his crooked yellow teeth because every time she brushed his teeth, he sneezed."

"So, all of the sentences after the first sentence elaborate upon the first idea in which Opal says, 'When I was done working on him, Winn-Dixie looked a whole lot better.' Could anyone remind us of what it means to elaborate?"

John raises his hand. "Add details."

"Yes. In fact, one dictionary defines *elaborate* as 'to add details to; to expand.' A simpler way of thinking about this is: elaborate means *to tell more*." I write this on a chart.

"After the first sentence, does Kate DiCamillo (through the character of Opal) *tell more* about the way Winn-Dixie now looks?"

Students answer, "Yes."

I continue, "She *tells what* problems he still has. She *tells how* she is going to help his ribs not show anymore. She *tells why* she could not do anything about his yellow teeth. She *tells where* she is taking the dog, now that he is cleaned up, and *tells who* they are going to see. All of these details *tell more* about the idea in her first sentence. That is elaboration of ideas!"

I stop and refer to a chart we made during our focus on narrowing topics, to remind us what it means to elaborate; see Figure 5.1.

FIGURE 5.1 *Ways to elaborate*

Tell more by:

- Telling what happened.
- Telling who was there.
- Telling how you felt.
- Telling what someone said.
- Telling why this time was memorable.

Teaching Tip

Make anchor charts with ideas that will help students in their writing. Keep these posted for students to use as a reference.

10 Essential Writing Lessons © 2013 by Megan Sloan, Scholastic Teaching Resources

I tell students that this chart will help us as we work to elaborate on our ideas. It will stay posted and will serve as a reminder of different ways we can *tell more*. I encourage students to look for ways authors elaborate as they read over the next week. If they find a specific way an author tells more (from our chart of ideas), I ask them to mark it with a sticky note so they can share with the class during our next writing lesson.

✳ Day Two: "Telling More"—Modeled Writing

I begin by sharing, "In our last lesson, we learned about ways authors elaborate on ideas." I direct students to our chart, and we discuss the various ways an author can *tell more*. I remind them, "When you write about an idea, think about the ways you can *tell more*. For instance, if I decide to write about my camping trip and I am writing a paragraph about making S'mores, I think about telling how I roasted the marshmallows, where I am, who I am with, when we did this in relation to the other things we did, and maybe add a sentence about why we made these treats."

> **Teaching Tip**
>
> Sometimes it is helpful to prepare your modeled writing before the lesson. This works when you want students to examine the piece closely, rather than see the process of drafting.

To save time you could choose to write a piece ahead of time and then share it during the lesson. This is a good option when time is short or you are worried about keeping the attention of students for a longer period. However, whenever possible, I prefer to write in front of students so they can hear me think aloud as I write. I have included my think-aloud comments below.

"I am going to write about something I love to do when we go camping." *I love roasting marshmallows and making S'mores.* "Let me say when we do it and what we will need." *After everyone has eaten hot dogs and the fire is still blazing, we take out the marshmallows, find the roasting sticks we brought along with us, and begin.* "Okay, I should tell what we do first." *First we poke the marshmallow onto the end of the sticks. We sit close to the heat and hold our sticks over the fire, turning them gently as the heat makes the marshmallows brown.*

"Now I am going to say how I like my marshmallows cooked, and then how my sister cooks hers." *I like my marshmallow to be light brown, but my sister always lets hers catch on fire. When it does, we all let out a scream and she blows out the flame. Her marshmallow now looks black, but she doesn't care.*

"Now the next step." *We slide the gooey messes onto our graham crackers, add a piece of chocolate and cap it off with another graham cracker. Then we take our first bite!* "Okay, now I need an ending sentence." *This is always the best part of camping.*

I let students work in pairs to talk about my main idea (making S'mores) and the ways I elaborated in my paragraph. Then we share with the whole class. Students decide I elaborated in the following ways:

- told who
- told what
- told why
- told where
- told how

Students have a conversation about this part: . . . *but my sister always lets hers catch on fire. When it does, we all let out a scream and she blows out the flame.* Bryan says, "It's like you are telling us a little story."

"You're right. It is kind of like a little story about what happened. We are going to learn about this on another day. This is a mini-anecdote—a story within a story."

✳ Day Three: "Telling More"—Independent Writing

I begin the next day by inviting students to write their own paragraph. I say, "I want you to choose a topic to write a paragraph about. The topic can be an experience you have had, something you know a lot about, or something you are interested in. You might want to look back at your topics lists in your writer's notebooks."

Students take time to choose topics and begin writing. During this time, I confer with individuals. Students read what they have so far, and we talk about specific ways they might *tell more.* I ask questions to promote elaboration of ideas.

For example, Hunter reads me what he has written so far.

> I went to the fair this summer. I had a great time. My favorite ride was the roller coaster. We rode it three times. I also like the pig races. They are funny to watch. We ate lots of junk food.

I tell Hunter, "It looks like you are off to a good start. However, I have some questions for you that might help you add some interesting details. Would you mind reading your writing again to me, and may I stop you when I have a question?"

"Sure," Hunter answers. He reads his first sentence. *I went to the fair this summer.*

"Okay, stop. What kind of day was it? Did you go in the day or in the evening?"

Hunter answers, "It was really hot that day, maybe the hottest day of the summer."

"Oh, I love that. How could you add that detail into your piece?" Hunter decides to add his new detail after the first sentence, so now it reads *I went to the fair this summer. It was really hot that day, maybe the hottest day of the summer.*

"Okay, continue." Hunter reads *I had a great time. My favorite ride was the roller coaster.*

"Stop. Why was the roller coaster your favorite ride?" I ask.

"It went really fast, and my stomach felt like it was flipping around when we went around the corners."

"Who rode with you?" I ask.

"My dad did. My mom and little sister wouldn't go on it. My dad and I put our hands up in the air like this (Hunter lifts his arms above his head to show me) when we zoomed down the hill part of the ride."

I comment, "Oh that is such great elaborating. I love these details. Would you like to add them to your writing?"

Hunter decides to add them, and now his piece reads:

> My favorite ride was the roller coaster. I went on it with my dad. My mom and little sister wouldn't go. When the roller coaster went around the corner, my stomach almost flipped. We held our arms up in the air when the roller coaster went down the hill. It was pretty scary. I screamed really loud.

I point out to Hunter that by asking questions like *What kind of day was it?, Who went with you?*, *Why did you like that ride best?*, he was able to elaborate with some very interesting details.

I go on to ask Hunter why he liked the pig races and what made them funny. He said, "The pigs kick up their hind legs, and sometimes the mud flies. Sometimes they slide in the mud, too. Everyone is cheering for them. The pig with the green vest won."

Clearly, by asking Hunter some simple questions, I am able to encourage him to add some relevant details. Before I leave to confer with another child, I encourage Hunter to ask himself these *what, where, who, how,* and *when* questions after he writes a sentence and see if it leads to any details he would like to add.

ELABORATING BY INCLUDING SENSORY DESCRIPTION

Our senses are how we observe the world around us. Writers use sight, sound, smell, taste, and touch to paint vivid pictures for readers. In order to teach description—using one's senses—as a strategy for elaborating on ideas, I begin by sharing a favorite mentor text or two, to show this in action.

✳ Day One: Sharing Mentor Texts to Explore Sensory Description

Choosing the right mentor texts is important. My first criterion for choosing a text for modeling is I have to love it. If I do not love the text, then it probably won't work well as a mentor for students. My second criterion is that I have to see something it can teach students about writing. This might include the use of interesting language, a good lead, elaborating on ideas, a strong character, or a satisfying ending. Once a text has met these two criteria, I must match it with what my students are ready to learn. If a text models an interesting way to elaborate on ideas, and that is what my students are learning to do, then it is a good mentor for that particular lesson. If we are working on interesting language, then I will choose a mentor text I love in which the author uses interesting words and phrasing.

> ### My Criteria for Choosing a Mentor Text
>
> 1. I have to love the text.
> 2. I have to see something the text can teach my students.
> 3. I have to match the text with what my students are ready to learn.

For this lesson, I gather students around me, and we reread a paragraph from our read-aloud, *Each Little Bird That Sings* by Deborah Wiles. This is a rich piece of writing with a strong character, complex story line, interesting details, and wonderful language. I set the book under the document camera, and we study how Wiles uses description to elaborate upon Listening Rock.

Listening Rock glittered where the quartz sparkled it. It pebbled and flaked in the limestone places. Here and there scrub pines and bushes jutted from the granite surface. Patches of daisies sprouted from the rock in sandy places, with a few determined bumblebees buzzing around them, but mostly there was wide, warm rock to walk on at a slow but steady rise. (p. 31)

We discuss the ways Wiles describes Listening Rock. We see the glittering flakes on the rock and the pines and bushes that jut out from the surface. We see the patches of daisies sprouting. We see and hear the bumblebees buzzing around, and we feel the warmth of the rock itself, as it slowly rises.

I tell students, "The author's description encourages readers to pause and be there, right on the rock with Comfort. She speaks to our senses. By writing with rich sensory details, she helps readers experience the moment as if they were actually there."

✳ Day Two: Including Sensory Description—Shared Writing

I ask students to get their writer's notebooks, and we head outside to a garden on our campus. (You may find some other place on or near your campus that will work for describing a place. It might be a bridge nearby, a fire station, a bird nest.)

We all find a place to perch where we can observe and think about the sights, sounds, smells, and feels of this place. I begin, "I notice the velvet reds and purples of the tulips. Who else notices something?"

Avery says, "There is a cool breeze blowing on my cheek."

Isabella adds, "I feel the sun on my face and arms."

> **Teaching Tip**
>
> Use chart paper for shared writing so you have a record of the work that students can refer to later.

I encourage students to write down their thoughts. We continue sharing ideas and writing them down in our notebooks for the next ten minutes. Then we return to class with ideas for our writing.

I guide students in a shared writing about our garden. I almost always use chart paper for shared writing. This way, our writing can stay up on the wall so we can refer to it later. "Okay, how should we begin?"

Ryan answers, "Today we sat in our beautiful school garden."

Right as he finishes, Claire suggests, "We should say 'our splendid garden.'"

I combine Ryan and Claire's ideas and record our first sentence.

"Okay, what's next?"

"Velvet red and purple tulips stand tall like they're saying hello," says Eleanor.

Josh adds, "An orange and black butterfly flutters to a flower, pauses, then opens its wings and flits away."

"Very nice," I respond. We continue sharing ideas, making little changes along the way, until we have a first draft of a paragraph.

Today we visit our splendid school garden. Velvet red and purple tulips stand tall like they are saying hello. An orange and black butterfly flutters to a flower, pauses, then opens its wings and flits away. Ivy ferns and emerald plants surround the tulips. A bee comes to visit, buzzing in our ears. The sun feels warm on our faces as we sit and enjoy this colorful place.

We read our paragraph together a couple of times to study our elaboration techniques. I ask, "What ways did we elaborate in our writing about our garden?"

Jesse says, "We describe the colors of the tulips."

Tatum adds, "We describe the color of the butterfly and tell what it does . . . it flutters on some flowers before it flits away."

"We use interesting 'green' words to describe the plants," says Aida.

"*Ivy* and *emerald*," adds Sydney.

"We say that we hear a bee buzzing," says Dylan.

Ryan says, "And we say we feel the warm sun on our faces."

"Yes. Just like Deborah Wiles' describes Listening Rock using her senses, we use our senses to describe our garden. By elaborating on our idea, we have invited our readers to pause and experience the moment."

Students Prepare to Write Independently

I begin, "I want you to find a place you like to visit over the next few days. Maybe it is a rock like Comfort or maybe it is the beach, your backyard, your kitchen, or even your bed. Take time to think about the sights, sounds, smells, tastes, and touches you experience there. Take notes in your writer's notebook. When we come back together, you will use your notes to write a longer piece."

✳ Day Three: Including Sensory Description— Independent Writing

Reece writing independently

We begin our next lesson on the carpet, writer's notebooks in laps. I invite students to share their writing. "The last couple of days you had a chance to find a small spot or place to sit. I asked you to observe the sights, sounds, smells, tastes, and textures around you and take a few notes about what you observed. Would anyone like to share their experience with us?"

Kaden begins, "Well, I sat in my kitchen while my mom was making dinner."

"Tell us more. What did you write down?"

Kaden reads from her notebook:

A pot clanks against another pot.
My mom is moving around, from the sink to the stove.
The refrigerator door is opening and closing.
I can smell the chicken in the oven.

"That's great. Let me ask you something. What sound is the refrigerator door making?" I am prompting Kaden here to think about more detailed sensory descriptions.

"It's like a slap," says Kaden.

I nod, "Now I can hear it."

A few more students share their places and ideas from their notebooks. Then I ask students to take a few moments to write a paragraph about their places. "Remember to elaborate using your senses."

At this time I sit with students one-on-one. I ask them to share their ideas and work with them to craft their paragraphs. As I did with Kaden, I ask students first about the place they are describing. Then I ask them to read me their descriptors. I prompt with clarifying questions like *What did that sound like?, Can you describe the size/color/shape of that?*, and *Did that taste/sound/sight remind you of anything else?* This helps students be as specific as possible.

Students pair up and read to each other. I encourage them to ask each other the same kinds of questions I asked Kaden. The goal is for students to use peer and teacher feedback to add, change, and edit their writing. Of course, this kind of peer work takes practice. It improves with more modeling and time.

FIGURE 5.2 *Kaden's paragraph*

Kitchen at Dinnertime

My kitchen is a warm place. Tonight my mom is bustling around as she cooks dinner. Chicken is in the oven. I can smell it along with the stuffing that is on the stove. My mom stops to stir the stuffing and the spoon clinks against the pan as she finishes. Then my mom opens the oven door. I hear a slight sizzling and then click, the door closes. My mom reaches for the refrigerator door handle and sluk—the door opens. She grabs the milk and begins to pour two glasses for my brother and me. The white bubbles up at the top of the glasses. "Take these to the table," my mom says. She returns the milk and I hear the refrigerator door slap shut. Then my mom says, "Go wash your hands. Dinner is almost ready."

Over the next few weeks, we notice other ways authors elaborate. We focus on several mentor texts and study authors' techniques. These are listed below in each of the elaboration sections.

ELABORATING BY INCLUDING ANECDOTES

According to *Webster's Dictionary*, an anecdote is a "short account of an interesting or amusing incident or event, often biographical." One of my goals is to teach students to include anecdotes in their writing. This is a rich and personal way to elaborate on ideas. Anecdotes reel readers further into the story they are reading.

✳ Day One: Sharing Mentor Texts to Discover Anecdotes

I recently read *Half Broke Horses* by Jeannette Walls. It is filled with many anecdotes, or what I like to call *stories within a story*. These anecdotes are jewels. The author not only uses them to elaborate on ideas, but includes them to make us feel like we are there with the real life characters she is writing about.

One such anecdote comes early in the book as Lily (Walls' grandmother) talks about playing baseball when they were kids.

. . . we made up a lot of our own rules, one being that you could get a runner out by throwing the ball at him. Once, when I was ten and trying to steal a base, one of the Dingler boys threw the ball at me hard and it hit me in the stomach. I doubled over, and when the pain wouldn't go away, Dad took me to Toyah, where the barber who sometimes sewed people up said my appendix had been ruptured and I needed to get up to the hospital in Santa Fe . . . . (p. 25)

I read this anecdote to students in its entirety, after sharing a brief description of the book. We talk about the way the author begins the "story within the story." Students note that Lily is talking about playing baseball and says they made up their own rules, "one being that you could get a runner out by throwing the ball at him." Then she says, "Once . . ." and tells about the time something interesting happened as a result of this rule: her appendix was burst because the ball hit her stomach hard.

We look for other examples of anecdotes in the books in our classroom. We notice most of them appear in memoirs, biographies, and autobiographies. This makes sense when we look back at the definition of an anecdote as being ". . . often biographical."

From: Time for Kids Biographies—*Harriet Tubman: A Woman of Courage*:

Harriet and her passengers had many close calls. On one rescue trip slave hunters were close behind her. They caught up with her and her passengers near a train station. Harriet had to think fast. She quickly pushed her passengers onto a train heading south. She knew the slave hunters would never look on that train. After all, runaway slaves wanted to go north, not south. The trick worked perfectly and the authorities paid no attention to them. (p. 23)

From: *Daniel Boone* by Candice Ransom:

Daniel rambled happily over the mountains. Sometimes he lay on the ground and sang at the top of his lungs. Once he left his mark on a tree. It said, "D. Boone killed a bear on tree in the year 1760." (p. 18)

From: *Who Was Louis Armstrong?* by Yona Zeldis McDonough:

It was not easy to be a young African-American boy in the early 1900s. Though slavery had ended in 1865, many white people thought blacks were not as good as white people . . . .

Once, Louis got on a streetcar . . . There were lots of empty seats up front, so Louis sat down. The babysitter told him to come back and sit with her. But Louis didn't want to . . . she got up and dragged him to the back . . . If she hadn't, all three of them could have been thrown off the bus . . . or even arrested. Seats in the front were for white people only.

Another time, Louis . . . (p. 8, p. 10)

I ask students, "What do you notice about the way each of these anecdotes begin? What word or words do the authors use?" I reread the sentences that begin each anecdote.

Edgar answers, "Once . . ."

Jayger adds, "Another time . . ."

"In the Harriet Tubman book, it says, 'On one rescue trip . . .'"

I write these on a chart of anecdote starters; see Figure 5.3. As we continue to discover other anecdotes in books, we add to the list.

✳ Day Two: Writing Anecdotes—Modeled and Independent Writing

We review what we learned the previous day about anecdotes. I tell students I am going to write about an experience I had growing up. I talk about being a gymnast and tell about all of the good times learning tricks and competing for awards. Then I tell students about the down side: Gymnastics can be dangerous because sometimes you get hurt.

As I tell my story, I begin to write. I think aloud and make revisions, adding words and sentences, and crossing out lines that don't work. After I write my first few sentences, I say to students, "I want to tell a little story here about one time when I really got hurt bad. I could begin, 'One time.'" I go on to write about my ankle injury.

> When I was growing up I was a gymnast. This sport was really difficult and a bit dangerous. I hurt my back and my knee. I even broke my toe. One time, I had just gotten back from a trip. I hadn't practiced in three weeks. I was on the beam and I decided to do a trick called a gainer. That's when you flip backward off of one foot to the side of the beam. There was a thick mat that was only half way under the beam. I thought it would be okay, so I started to dismount and I went out further than I usually do. My right foot landed half way off the mat. I twisted my ankle. I remember the pain was so bad I couldn't speak. It swelled up like a grapefruit that night, and I ended up in the emergency room the next morning. I was in a cast for four weeks and later on had surgery. From then on, I always made sure the mat was pulled all the way under the beam.

When I am finished, we talk about how my anecdote works to elaborate on my idea that gymnastics can be dangerous because you can get hurt.

Students Write Anecdotes

I then ask students to think about a sport or activity they do about which they can tell a "One time . . ." story. Alternatively, they can think about a special place they visit a lot, a holiday, or vacation. There might be an "I remember one time . . ." or a "My favorite time was . . ." story they could share.

Students share possible topics with the group, and I send them to write when I think they are ready with some ideas. Again, I wander the room and confer with students, helping them focus in on a topic, add sentences to elaborate, and include at least one anecdote.

Anecdote Starters...
- Once
- One time
- Another time
- I remember when
- One day
- Sometimes
- My favorite time was
- I remember once

FIGURE 5.3 *Student-generated list of anecdote starters*

Examples, statistics, and definitions are three more ways authors elaborate on ideas in text. While all three are used in fiction, they are also found in nonfiction texts, so I often begin these lessons when we might be getting ready to dive into informational writing.

✳ Day One and Beyond: Sharing Mentor Texts

I begin sharing texts that show the use of examples, statistics, and definitions. We talk informally about how these help to elaborate on authors' ideas. I read picture books, parts of chapter books, *Scholastic News*, as well as other articles from newspapers and magazines. I encourage students to go on "hunts" for these techniques in the texts they are reading. This exploration may last awhile. Here are some examples I have used with my students.

Examples

From: *Frogs* by Nic Bishop

> A few frogs, such as wood frogs and spring peepers, will even freeze partly solid. (p. 30)

From: *Honus and Me* by Dan Gutman

> Being a collector and all, I couldn't resist peeking into a few of Miss Young's old boxes to see what kind of stuff she had decided to hang onto all these years. But it was exactly what she said it was—worthless junk. Broken candlesticks. Old clothes. A set of encyclopedias. I chucked it all out. (p. 15)

From: *Charlotte's Web* by E. B. White

> A fair is a rat's paradise. Everybody spills food at a fair. A rat can creep out late at night and have a feast. In the horse barn you will find oats that the trotters and pacers have spilled. In the trampled grass of the infield you will find old discarded lunch boxes containing the foul remains of peanut butter sandwiches, hard-boiled eggs, cracker crumbs, bits of doughnuts, and particles of cheese. (pp. 122–123)

From: *Sitting Bull* by Susan Bivin Aller

> To force the Plains Indians onto reservations, the government decided to get rid of the buffalo. It hired sharpshooters, people who were skilled at shooting targets, to kill the buffalo. Between 1872 and 1874, these sharpshooters killed more than four million of the animals. By 1895, fewer than one thousand buffalo were left. (p. 33)

I love playing baseball. It is one of my favorite sports. My team is The White Sox. We have played together for a couple of years. Baseball can be really scary at times because sometimes it is all up to you. If you hit the ball, you win and you are the hero. If you strike out, you lose and you feel awful.

I remember two summers ago when I was in that position. It was the championship game and everyone was there watching: my mom, dad, grandparents, and brother. We had been ahead, but then in the last inning, the other team scored and we were down 6 to 5. We were up to bat. There were two kids on base but then the next two guys got out. I was the last one who could help us win. I was really nervous as I stepped to the plate. My palms were sweaty and I was thinking, "I need to hit this ball good." I looked at the pitcher real hard and stared him down. I took two practice swings and stood there hoping I could hit it. First pitch—Strike one! I waited for it to come right over the plate.

I knew everyone was watching. I swung and the ball flew out over the second baseman. I ran like lightning to first base. The other two guys took off and made it to home plate. I was so happy. I could now breathe. We won the game. I will always remember that nerve-racking time at the plate.

FIGURE 5.4 *Ryan elaborates by using an anecdote.*

Statistics

From: *Everest: Reaching for the Sky* by Joy Masoff

> The trip to the top of Everest is full of danger. For one thing, it is bitter cold. Temperatures can drop to minus 40 degrees F . . . Winds can blow as hard as a hurricane with gusts up to 120 miles (193 kilometers) per hour. (p. 8)

From: *Honus and Me* by Dan Gutman

> Despite his size he could run like a scared rabbit. Wagner stole 722 bases over his career, and led the league in stolen bases five times. (p. 27)

Definitions

From: *Eleanor Roosevelt* by Mary Winget

> On their travels, Eleanor and Franklin saw how the Great Depression, a long period of hard times, was affecting the country. (p. 24)

From: *Nubs: The True Story of a Mutt, a Marine, and a Miracle* by Brian Dennis, Mary Nethery, and Kirby Larson

> Brian tightened his winter scarf, a Keffiyah, around his neck and then climbed inside the Humvee.

We make charts of key words or phrases that might indicate when an author is using an example, statistic, or definition as a way to elaborate and make the text more meaningful; see Figure 5.5. The charts serve as references for students as they think about using these techniques to elaborate in their writing.

Examples

- for instance
- for example
- such as
- like
- the use of a colon

Statistics

- the use of numbers to indicate speed, height, weight, temperature, length of time, etc.

Definition

- this means
- a _____ is
- this is
- the use of an appositive (a clause that defines a word and is set off by commas)

FIGURE 5.5
Class chart summarizing how writers introduce examples, statistics, and definitions.

 10 Essential Writing Lessons © 2013 by Megan Sloan, Scholastic Teaching Resources

✳ Days That Follow: Shared Writing

During our Reader's Workshop students become interested in studying different kinds of natural disasters. We observe the weather and natural disasters that have occurred around the world over the last year. We note areas that have experienced tornadoes, hurricanes, blizzards, earthquakes, tsunamis, and more.

Students form groups of four to study their chosen natural disasters. They collect many books and other texts from the classroom, library, and home. They read, take notes, and then decide to write a class book, with each small group of students responsible for the section on their natural disaster. See one group's writing on tornadoes in Figure 5.6.

As they take notes, I encourage students to collect statistics and examples. I also suggest they keep in mind any words they might need to define. When students begin drafting, I also give several reminders to include leads, elaborate on ideas using the techniques we have studied, and include ending sentences or paragraphs.

FIGURE 5.6 *Student page on tornadoes*

Tornadoes

Tornadoes are fierce storms that can do tons of damage to anything in their way. Tornadoes are also known as twisters. They produce the fastest and strongest winds on Earth. Their winds can be as strong as 300 mph. Some tornadoes last a few minutes and some last a much longer time, traveling across the land for hours.

Tornadoes are so powerful. They can lift trailer trucks and toss them around like toys. They can tear roofs off houses and bend huge trees and break them into pieces.

Tornadoes start as warm, humid air. This warm air meets colder air. As the two temperatures come together they cause the warm air to rise and produce huge, dark clouds called **thunderheads**. These thunderheads cause giant storms with thunder and lightning called **supercells**. The winds begin to spin and form a long **funnel cloud**. When the funnel cloud touches the ground, it becomes a tornado.

Three out of every four tornadoes happen in the United States. There are about 800 tornadoes every year here. Some people chase tornadoes. This is not a good idea. You can really get hurt. It is better to go down to a basement or hide in your bathtub and wait for the storm to pass.

✳ Final Thoughts

Students now have experience with several elaboration techniques. They find these techniques in mentor texts. They see elaboration modeled in front of them, as well as have the support of other writers as they compose shared writing pieces. Now it is their turn to take the leap and experiment with different ways to elaborate. They might not be perfect at first, but it is all about giving it a try. The more students practice a writing strategy, the more likely they will be to add this strategy to their writing toolbox.

Writing Poetry: Learning About Language and Developing Confidence

I have always loved reading poetry to and with students. Even in my early years of teaching, I incorporated reading poetry into each day. But when it came to writing poetry, it was a different story. I struggled to teach my students to write poetry that was more than just attempts at putting a bunch of rhyming words together that didn't really make much sense. So, like many teachers, I waited to teach students to write poetry until the end of the year, hoping they had mastered skills to make the process more successful.

Then, quite a few years ago, I decided to begin the year with writing poetry, using it to teach topic choice and to launch the writer's notebook. I jumped in, sharing lots of poems with my students and teaching them about free verse. Students had opportunities to observe and make lists. I modeled the process for them, and we wrote lots of poems together. I worked with small groups of students and met with them one-on-one. I began to see incredible learning happening, particularly with my struggling writers. What I found changed my thinking about students and writing poetry. I observed two things occurring:

1. Struggling writers find success in writing poetry because a) poems can be short, and b) poems don't have to be written in complete sentences. Consequently, struggling writers (as well as ELL students) find confidence as writers. They become writers by becoming poets. They are celebrated for their success in writing poetry and now have the confidence to believe they can write other genres.

2. Students learn about phrasing and elements of language (metaphor, simile, alliteration) by writing poetry. Consequently, they write in other genres, such as narrative, expository, and persuasive, with added fluency.

In addition to these two findings, I observed my students' vocabulary growing by leaps and bounds. Regie Routman says, "One of the best things about poetry is that kids get to play around with language and have fun with it. Such playfulness helps develop children's interest in language, which carries over to other forms of writing" (2005, p. 31). She goes on to add, "Of all the writing I have ever done with students, poetry brings the most joy, ease, and success for both students and teachers."

While poetry is not a specific text type included in the Common Core State Standards for writing, Writing Standard 3 for grades 3–5 does ask students to "develop experiences or events using effective technique, *descriptive details*, and clear event sequences" (italics added); in grades 4 and 5, the standards specifically ask students to "use concrete words and phrases and sensory details to convey experiences and events precisely" (Writing Standard 3d). Writing poetry fosters these skills. In addition, The Reading Standard for Literature 10 requires students in grades 3–5 to read and comprehend a range of literature, including poetry. Anchor Standard 4 for Reading states that students should be able to "Interpret words and phrases as they are used in a text, including determining technical, connotative, and figurative meanings, and analyze how specific word choices shape meaning or tone." Reading and writing poetry, as we do in this unit, develops essential skills students need to meet these standards.

I have come to believe that teaching students to write poetry should not be an "add on" unit at the end of the year, if time allows. It could begin the year, as a text type during lessons on the writer's notebook or discovering topics, and it can be part of student writing (and reading) lessons throughout the year.

✳ Sharing Poetry

Before students begin writing poetry, they need to hear it read aloud. I start our lessons by reading aloud all kinds of poems by varying poets: Douglas Florian, Rebecca Kai Dotlich, Sara Holbrook, Shel Silverstein, Joyce Sidman, Eloise Greenfield, and many more. We talk about the topics and enjoy the language. Students echo read, and we also do lots of popcorn reading, assigning lines to individual students. Sometimes we trade off with girls reading a line, boys reading a line. I want students to feel the joy of poetry.

✳ Day One: Recording Favorite Lines

After we have shared many poems, I tell students, "Today I am going to share a few of my favorites." I project them one at a time on the board and read aloud to students. I begin with "Wonder Through the Pages" by Karla Kuskin, found in *I Am the Book*, poems selected by Lee Bennett Hopkins. I read the poem once, asking students to listen carefully. Then I read the poem a second time and ask students to take note of any favorite words or lines.

When I finish, I ask, "So, did any of you hear a line you really liked?"

Jada says, "*nonsense and knowledge*."

Hunter adds, "That's alliteration."

I answer, "Yes it is. What sounds do you hear at the beginning of both of those words?"

Jada responds, "n."

Ryan says, "I like *wisdom of wizards*."

I respond, "That is also an example of alliteration. It's really fun to say that line. Let's all say it." Students repeat the line aloud. "Why did you like that line, Ryan?"

Ryan says, "I like the sound of it, and also I like that the poet is saying wizards are wise."

I continue, "Are there any other lines you like?"

Isabella says, "*whispering mysteries.*"

I prod, "What do you like about that line?"

Isabella answers, "It's like there's a mystery and someone is quietly whispering it to us, like when you read a book there are mysteries slowly unfolding."

"I understand what you are saying. Let's read the poem together." We read the poem again and again, in a variety of ways.

- Boys read one line, girls read the next.
- Popcorn poetry—Everyone reads the title, and then individual students take a line.
- Echo reading—I read a line, students echo me.

I project another poem on the board, and we repeat the process. This time I choose an acrostic poem that does not rhyme. It is titled "Hummingbird" in a book of poems called *Silver Seeds* by Paul Paolilli and Dan Brewer. Students read aloud and share lines they like. If time permits, we read and share even more poems, listening to and appreciating the language and rhythm. I've included a list of my favorite poetry books below.

List of Some of My Favorite Poetry Books

- *A Writing Kind of Day: Poems for Young Poets* by Ralph Fletcher
- *All the Small Poems and Fourteen More* by Valerie Worth
- *Baseball, Snakes, and Summer Squash: Poems About Growing Up* by Donald Graves
- *Color Me a Rhyme: Nature Poems for Young People* by Jane Yolen
- *Dark Emperor and Other Poems of the Night* by Joyce Sidman
- *Doodle Dandies: Poems That Take Shape* by J. Patrick Lewis
- *Extra Innings: Baseball Poems* selected by Lee Bennett Hopkins
- *Good Books, Good Times!* selected by Lee Bennett Hopkins
- *Haiku Hike* by the fourth-grade students of St. Mary's Catholic School in Mansfield, Massachusetts
- *Handsprings* by Douglas Florian
- *Honey, I Love and Other Love Poems* by Eloise Greenfield
- *I Am the Book* selected by Lee Bennett Hopkins
- *Insectlopedia* by Douglas Florian
- *Lemonade Sun: And Other Summer Poems* by Rebecca Kai Dotlich
- *Once I Ate a Pie* by Patricia MacLachlan and Emily MacLachlan Charest
- *One Leaf Rides the Wind* by Celeste Davidson Mannis
- *Shape Me a Poem: Nature's Forms in Poetry* by Jane Yolen
- *Sharing the Seasons: A Book of Poems* selected by Lee Bennett Hopkins
- *Silver Seeds: A Book of Nature Poems* by Paul Paolilli and Dan Brewer
- *This Is Just to Say: Poems of Apology and Forgiveness* by Joyce Sidman
- *Under the Sunday Tree* by Eloise Greenfield
- *Winter Eyes* by Douglas Florian

✳ Day Two: Exploring Poetry: What Do We Notice?

As we continue to share poetry aloud, I encourage students to find at least one or two poetry books from our classroom (or the library) to keep in their book boxes. Every day they read alone and with friends from their books. They trade and recommend books to each other. They mark pages with sticky notes to share later with a friend or the entire class. After a couple of weeks, we stop to review what we have learned.

Teaching Tip

Let students read and explore poetry before writing.

"We have been reading lots of poems over the last couple of weeks. What have you noticed about poetry? I thought it would be helpful if we recorded our thinking. So, as you share ideas, I am going to type and project them onto our SMARTBoard®."

Ryan offers, "Poems can be funny."

"Yes. Which poets write funny poems?"

Makenzie says, "Shel Silverstein and Douglas Florian."

"Jack Prelutsky," adds Fernando.

I continue, "What else do you notice about poems?"

"They can be about anything," says Jean.

"Okay. Like what?"

Jean answers, "Well, some are about nature and some are about sports."

Ryan adds, "Or people. I read one about Ben Franklin the other day."

Tyler adds, "Shel Silverstein wrote one about a little sister."

"I have a whole book of poems about insects," says Hannah.

Maddy holds up her two books and says, "This one is all about the seasons, and this one is about colors."

I respond, "We could probably list more than 100 topics poets write about in no time at all. What else do you notice about poetry?"

Juan adds, "Some poems rhyme and some don't."

"You are right. Some poets write rhyming poems while others write what we call free verse, or non-rhyming poems. I like both kinds. How about you?"

Fernando nods, "Both."

Students reading poetry

Students continue to share as I record their ideas. We end up with a lengthy list of observations about poetry (see Figure 6.1). This list serves as a foundation for students as they embark on writing poetry next.

FIGURE 6.1 *Our class-generated list about poetry*

What We Notice About Poetry

- Poems can be funny.
- Poems can be about anything (like nature or sports or people).
- Some poems rhyme and some don't.
- Poems include interesting vocabulary.
- Poems include simile, metaphor, and alliteration.
- Poems can make us happy, sad, laugh, cry, or tug at our heart.
- The lines in poems don't always go to the end of the line.
- There is a lot of white space on the page.
- Poems can be short or long.
- Poems usually have titles.
- Poems include words we don't always know.
- There are different kinds of poems, like haiku, free verse, rhyming, limerick, and shape poems.
- Poems can inspire you.
- Poems can tell real information.
- Poems are fun to read aloud.
- Poems are not to be read only once.
- Poems are fun to read with a friend.
- Poems can make us want to write poems.
- Sometimes poems are anonymous.

✳ Day Three: Discovering Found Poetry

To teach the idea of phrase versus sentence, and the use of lovely language, I decide to share several picture books over the next few days; you'll find a list of my favorites on pages 63. I also continue to read our current chapter book, *Love, Ruby Lavender* by Deborah Wiles. I ask students to listen for lines that sound like poetry. I say, "Sometimes I am reading a nonfiction or fiction book, and I come across a line that sounds like a line from a poem. Today, I want you to listen for any lines that sound like poetry to you. A friend of mine calls this 'found poetry' because you find it in a genre other than a poem, so it's like a surprise find."

10 Essential Writing Lessons © 2013 by Megan Sloan, Scholastic Teaching Resources

Picture Books With Lovely Language or Lines of Found Poetry

- *A Grand Old Tree* by Mary Newell DePalma
- *All the Places to Love* by Patricia MacLachlan
- *Amber on the Mountain* by Tony Johnston
- *Aunt Harriet's Underground Railroad in the Sky* by Faith Ringgold
- *Duke Ellington* by Andrea Pinkney
- *The Eyes of Gray Wolf* by Jonathan London
- *First Snow in the Woods* by Carl R. Sams, II and Jean Stoick
- *Fox* by Margaret Wild
- *Hello Ocean* by Pam Muñoz Ryan
- *In November* by Cynthia Rylant
- *My Name Is Georgia* by Jeanette Winter
- *Owl Moon* by Jane Yolen
- *Pumpkin Circle: The Story of a Garden* by George Levenson
- *Walk With a Wolf* by Janni Howker
- *Where Once There Was a Wood* by Denise Fleming

Today I choose to read *Pumpkin Circle: The Story of a Garden* by George Levenson. I introduce the book to students, holding it up while asking, "What genre do you suppose this book is?"

Jayla says, "Well it kind of looks like nonfiction because there is a real photograph on the cover. But I don't know for sure."

I continue, "Let me show you just a few pages." I open the book to three various pages for students to take a quick look.

Trent says, "I think it is nonfiction, too. There are a lot of real photographs."

"Well, you both are right. This is a nonfiction book. But there is something really special about how the book is written. It almost sounds like a poem at times. There are a lot of lines that sound like poetry to me."

I invite students to open up their notebooks and listen carefully as I read. "When you hear a line that sounds like poetry, let me know with a smile or a thumbs up. Then write it down in your notebook."

I begin, and it doesn't take long before students are identifying lines that sound like poetry. I record their sharing on a chart.

This chart stays up in the room. We make a new chart, recording lines from other books we read together. Students are welcome to record lines they find during their own reading of different genres. In fact, I challenge students to be "Found Poetry Detectives" as they read during the day. Our new chart reminds us of all the lovely lines or "found poetry" in biographies, fiction, nonfiction, folktales, and other genres we read. See our discoveries in Figures 6.2 and 6.3.

Lines from: Pumpkin Circle

- Velvet petals open brilliant sunlit bowls.

- Twisty tendrils grasp like hands stretching out to cling.

- Pumpkins climbing up the fences.

- Here comes the harvest. Pluck treasures from the vine.

Found Poetry

~ "twisty tendrils grasp like hands
   Pumpkin Circle

~ "In a morning meadow far away, fog tiptoed in without a sound."
   First Snow in the Woods

~ "Lash, lunge, herons plunge."
   In a Small, Small Pond

~ "I walked down in the canyons of steel."
   My Name is Georgia

~ "She basked in the sun, bathed in the rain. swayed in the breeze. and danced in the wind."
   A Grand Old Tree

FIGURE 6.2 *Chart: Lines from Pumpkin Circle*

FIGURE 6.3 *Chart of "Found Poetry"*

✳ Day Four: Using a Mentor Text to Inspire Poets

I decide to share one of my favorite poetry books: *Color Me a Rhyme* by Jane Yolen. I open the book and read from the author's note at the beginning, where Yolen explains that her poems were inspired by photographs of nature. She looked for dominant colors and wrote these poems. She speaks directly to students when she says, "You can write poems from his (Jason Stemple's) photos, too. And as an added incentive, I have included extra "color" words to help you."

I begin reading the poems to students. We stop to discuss the photographs and the poems. We examine the color words the author includes for each color. I begin, "Wow! This photograph for her orange poem is incredible. The sunset through the clouds is stunning. And the orange on the rocks below is also interesting." I read the synonyms for *orange* that border the page: *pumpkin, copper, carrot, apricot, tangerine.*

"Let's see if we can come up with some poetic lines to describe this photo, using these synonyms for *orange*." I suggest, "Copper clouds race across the sky."

Joey says, "Pumpkin pulp sits on the rough rocks below."

I respond, "That's great. Anyone else?"

Jordan adds, "A fiery sunset captures the clouds as they try to escape."

I offer encouragement, "You are great at this. Let's go to another page." We turn to the Yellow poem. On one side is a photo of a tree in the forest filled with yellow leaves. On the other side is a close-up of a yellow leaf hanging off a branch of the tree. We read the two short poems and then read the synonyms for yellow that the author includes on the borders of the page: *canary, saffron, lemon, gold, flax, straw.*

Again, I invite students to share lines that might describe one of these photos, using a synonym for yellow.

Annaliese volunteers, "A lemon leaf dangles from a crooked branch."

I respond, "Oh, that is lovely. Isn't that lovely? Who else has a line?"

Jake says, "There's not much time before this saffron heart drops."

"Wow! You are all so poetic."

We continue turning the pages, reading the poems that go with each color and photograph. Students enjoy sharing lines, trying out the synonyms for each color. One of my goals in having students share lines orally is to experience putting words together to create just one phrase. This is do-able for some students who might struggle if I started with having them write a whole poem first. It also gives all of us a chance to really "hear" poetic lines, using the words Yolen encourages us to use.

✳ Day Five: Writing Poetry—Shared Writing

I begin this lesson by taking students out to a garden on our campus. We have been here before to observe this place. I encourage students to bring their notebooks and write down any observations they make. We talk as we walk around, sharing our observations. I take photographs of red and purple tulips and daffodils leaning up against each other. I take a close-up of one flower and a wide view of the entire garden. Students take their time observing this small place.

We come back to the room, and I immediately download the pictures I took. I print several of them for use during our writing lesson. I gather students together, and we choose a picture to inspire the shared poem we will write. The picture shows a close-up of two daffodils leaning up against each other (see the photo at right).

I also prepare a list of "yellow words" from Jane Yolen's book. As we begin to craft our poem, I share with students that even though we have many "yellow" words we can use, we don't want to overdo it. "Poets choose specific words to tell their stories. We may want to use just one or two of these yellow words in our poem about our daffodil picture. That way, they will stand out."

"Okay, let's begin. What do we notice about these daffodils?"

Jayger says, "They look like friends."

Reece adds, "They are leaning in to each other like they are whispering to each other."

I respond, "We have two really good ideas. Let me record those on our chart so we remember." I record both ideas on chart paper.

Trent says, "I wonder what they are whispering?"

"Me too. Do any of you have notes from your observations out there that we might use in our poem?"

Daesha says, "There was a soft breeze and the flowers were nodding."

Jayger adds, "They are popping up in the garden."

Daffodils in our garden

I record both ideas. "Okay. Let's try to take our ideas and write a poem about this photograph. How should we begin? What yellow word would we like to use in our poem?"

Rashana says, "I like *lemon*."

"Okay." I begin the poem. "How about *lemon friends*? They look like friends, don't you think?"

Students agree to begin the poem this way. They add lines using the ideas students shared earlier. We reread as we go. We cross out words and revise. We look to our green words and settle on *emerald* when describing the garden. Our final poem is shown in Figure 6.4.

FIGURE 6.4 *Final draft of "Lemon Friends"*

Lemon Friends

Lemon friends
growing in
an emerald
garden,
Popping up to
whisper a spring
hello to
all who pass
by. Their visit
here will not last
long. But, oh
how glorious
a visit it shall be.

Teaching Tip

Involve students in shared writing to develop confidence before they write on their own.

Students decide to write a second poem about the same photograph. Figure 6.5 shows our draft and final versions of "Saffron Gems."

FIGURE 6.5 *Draft and final version of our poem "Saffron Gems"*

Yellow   Draft

Saffron gems
leaning in to
~~whisper~~ tell a secret
in the
gentle
Spring
breeze.
What are they whispering?
These golden friends.

Saffron Gems

Saffron gems
leaning in to tell a secret,
in the gentle
spring breeze.
What are they whispering?
These golden forever friends.

We read our poems again, and I say, "Remember when we made our list of what we notice about poetry." I project our list on the board. "What do you notice about our first poem?"

Jenna says, "It has a yellow word in it."

"It's short," says John. "And it doesn't go all the way across the page."

Isabella adds, "I like the ending. It feels like the poem is finished."

"We used some interesting words, like *glorious* and *popping up*," says Trent.

"What do you notice about our second poem?"

Teddy says, "It's short."

"It has a question in it," adds Sofie.

Maddy says, "We used two yellow words."

"There's a lot of white space."

"It is about something in nature."

I do this activity so students can see that our poems have some of the same features we notice in the published poems in our classroom.

✳ Day Six: Writing Poetry—Independent Writing

I am very excited today because students will now have a chance to write their own poems. I bring out *Color Me a Rhyme* so students can be inspired by these photos. In addition, I have the pictures we took of our garden earlier, and I also have lots of pictures of nature from old National Geographic calendars I saved. I tear out photographs that seem to have a dominant color. Among them are pictures of red rock formations from the southwest, a green forest with a purple flower growing among the ferns, a white span of ice with one lonely polar bear crossing it. (Greeting cards with photographs on the front also work for this project. Another option is to take your own photographs of nature during all seasons and print them for students to use.)

Color word lists

I prepare lists of the color words. I write all of the yellow words on yellow paper, the green words on green, and so on. This helps students remember that *scarlet* is a red word, *canary* is a yellow word, and *azure* is a blue word.

Before we begin, I gather students and encourage them to choose a picture they really like, one that inspires them. I say, "You are going to write a poem about your picture, just like Jane Yolen did in her book *Color Me a Rhyme* and just like we did yesterday when we wrote "Saffron Gems." Remember to choose just a few words from the color words. Maybe your picture is mostly white, so you will just need the white words. Maybe you have green and white in your picture, and you'll also need the green words. I have written the color words on large paper that you can share. I also have them projected on the board. I will come around and talk to you as you are writing. Have fun!"

Conferring With Tatum and Corwin

I begin to wander around the room, helping students choose pictures and find the words they may want to use. I notice Tatum has chosen the picture of a wide span of ice with a small polar bear walking across it. I say, "Tell me about your picture."

Tatum says, "Well, the polar bear looks lonely. He's so small in this picture."

"I agree. The span of ice is so huge. Do you know how you want to start?"

Tatum says, "Yes. The ice looks like chalk. And I saw this word in another book that means lonely. It's *lone*." She takes out a book of haiku where the poet used *lone* to describe a snowman. "I think I want to use that to describe the polar bear."

"I think using the word *lone* is a great idea. Writers take note of words they like when they read and then they use them in their writing. It looks like you are off to a really good start. I will come back and check on you."

Next I stop at Corwin's side. He has a picture from Yolen's book in front of him. It shows a close-up of a branch with small green leaves and red berries. Corwin struggles with writing. He does not feel like a writer and has not had much success up to this point. But I see that he has started writing so I let him be for a few minutes; see his draft in Figure 6.6. I don't want to interrupt. He is usually a student who needs me to help him get started and this is the first time he has begun to write on his own—a real celebration!

FIGURE 6.6
Corwin's draft

After brief conversations with two other students, I come back to Corwin and am encouraged to see that he has written his poem. He shares it with me. Though it is short, it is amazing! I celebrate with Corwin. This is one of the first pieces he has taken pride in writing. I make sure he shares with the entire class, and even with former teachers' classes. Corwin is on his way!

FIGURE 6.7 *Corwin's final poem*

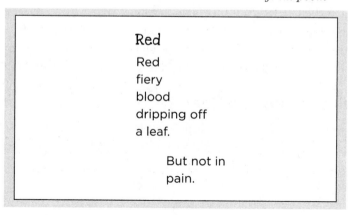

Red

Red
fiery
blood
dripping off
a leaf.

But not in
pain.

10 Essential Writing Lessons © 2013 by Megan Sloan, Scholastic Teaching Resources

Sharing Poetry

Students continue writing. Some finish one poem and write another, switching out pictures. I stop the group and encourage students to share with a peer. This actually is already happening. Students are excited and are feeling successful. I observe students helping each other to find just the right word.

Teaching Tip

Peer feedback can be very powerful for writers. Teach students to be positive, but also honest and helpful.

As students complete their drafts, I gather them together. They bring their photographs and first drafts. Students are eager to share their poems. I have them place them under the document camera so we can see the form the poem takes. Classmates make comments and ask questions. Some make suggestions about whether there are too many words on a line or too few. Some encourage the writer to use a different word or to add a line. Eddy suggested a classmate repeat a word because he thought it was important. During these comments, questions, and suggestions, I encourage the writer to listen to the advice and, if it is something he or she agrees with, make the change. If not, don't make the change. I say, "You are the writer. You get to make the final decision, but sometimes those who listen to your work have helpful advice. They are rooting for your poem to be the best it can be."

* Day Seven: Revising, Editing, and Publishing Poetry

I ask students to pair up to help each other make final revisions. Students revised a lot while they wrote, but today they take a fresh look at their poems and see if there are any changes to be made. I observe Isabella sharing her poem with Emma and listen in.

Isabella reads her poem inspired by a palm tree standing on a beautiful beach with blue water in the background. Emma says, "I really like your poem, but I think you might have too many green words in it. You have *olive, forest,* and *emerald* to describe the palm tree. Maybe you should pick your favorite green word and then it will stand out."

Isabella asks, "Which green word do you like best?"

Emma says, "I think you should pick your favorite."

Isabella decides, "I think I like *olive*."

Emma says, "I think that is a really good choice because the palm tree is kind of an olive green."

I also ask students to edit each others' poems. I encourage the use of dictionaries and/or spelling cards. I serve as a master editor, when needed. Students read their work and make final changes. Partners are expected to ask questions and make suggestions. I remind students, "We are all poets and we support one another, so have a listening ear if your partner makes a suggestion."

Students then take turns typing their poems. We print them, reread, make any last changes and retype if needed. Then we share our poems and the photographs that inspired them with the school. See Tatum's "White" poem in Figure 6.8 on page 70.

White

Snowy chalk
lays quietly and
wet
but only
the lone
polar bear
sees the
beauty.

✳ Lesson Extensions: More Independent Writing With Poetry

Even when this lesson is over, students have the opportunity to write more color poems inspired by photographs of nature. I keep the color word lists and the photographs in a folder. These stay in a tub, and students continue to choose to write color poems over the next few months, when they want to. In addition, I begin taking photographs of other things, like steps covered by autumn leaves or my niece up to bat at a baseball game. I encourage students to become photographers, too. They bring in pictures they take, and we add them to our folder. One child took a picture of a small green frog on a branch, and we all wrote a poem about it to open our writing workshop one day.

✳ Final Thoughts

While many poetry books were shared in these mini-lessons, and lots of observations about poems were made by students, I included only one mini-lesson in drafting poetry, using one mentor text. Of course, I hope this inspires teachers to try other lessons in teaching students to write all kinds of poetry based on observations of the world around them. Start with list poems and move onto other free verse about topics that matter to students. Encourage observations of the world as inspiration for writing poetry. Have students use their writer's notebooks to jot down those observations. Try different forms like haiku, acrostic, and shape poems. Read lots of poems aloud, model for students, engage students in shared writing, and finally, let students give writing poetry a try on their own.

Writing a Literary Essay

Literary essays are often required of students in middle and high school language arts classes. Essays of this sort usually ask students to examine an element of a story. For instance, students may analyze the setting, plot, character, or theme of a story. In doing so, they become critical thinkers about what they are reading. Practice with this kind of writing in the elementary grades not only helps students prepare for what is ahead, but also connects writing with reading and helps students better understand the elements of the stories they read.

✳ Sharing Mentor Texts

Before asking students to write about their reading in the form of a literary essay, we must first share many mentor texts and talk about elements of stories. These mentor texts come from the chapter read-alouds, as well as the multiple picture books teachers read to students each week. Stopping to talk about story elements during the reading of these texts will give students the support they need when they begin this writing unit. Students should have a clear understanding of plot before they are asked to analyze the plot of a story. Students should have multiple opportunities to discuss theme (and how it differs from "topic") before they are asked to analyze the theme of a story. Scaffolding is very important here. Teacher support and slow release of responsibility will make for a successful experience for students.

> **Teaching Tip**
>
> The chapter read-aloud works as a great mentor text for teaching writing.

For the purpose of modeling how to write a literary essay, I begin by focusing on character. I choose this story element because my students have been reading many stories that involve strong but diverse characters, which makes focusing on character a natural starting point for learning to write a literary essay.

✳ Day One: Using Mentor Texts to Introduce Literary Elements: Character

Discussions about *character* are not new for my students. We often stop to analyze the characters in the stories we read. I list some of my favorite books with strong character in the box below. We offer words to describe them and to talk about what motivates them to do what they do and say what they say. We predict and analyze the effects of their words and actions.

As we start this study, I open the discussion by asking students, "Who are some of our favorite or unforgettable characters from the stories we have read so far this year?" Many hands go up and students begin sharing.

"Poppy."

"Judy Moody."

"Alia Mohammed from *The Librarian of Basra*."

"Ereth from *Poppy*."

"The Centipede from *James and the Giant Peach*."

"Ruby Lavender."

"Stanley from *Holes*."

"Ivan from *The One and Only Ivan*."

I invite students to take a few minutes and look around the room. "Are there characters in books you read last year or the year before that are favorites?"

Students come back together with more characters to share.

"Charlotte and Wilbur from *Charlotte's Web*."

"Harry Potter."

"Sophie from *Sophie and Lou*."

"Despereaux from *The Tale of Despereaux*."

"Joe Stoshak from *Honus and Me*."

"Jack and Annie from the Magic Treehouse series."

I ask students, "What makes these characters our favorites? Why can't we forget about them?"

Eduardo answers, "They make the book interesting."

Ryan adds, "Yeah. It's like the book wouldn't be the same without them."

"Okay," I say. "What words would you use to describe some of these characters? You don't have to match your word with a character, although that might help, but what adjectives might tell us about at least one of the characters up here?"

Students begin to share adjectives, and I record them on chart paper; see Figure 7.1.

> ### Books With Strong and Unforgettable Characters
>
> - *Hatchet* by Gary Paulson
> - *Holes* by Louis Sachar
> - *The One and Only Ivan* by Katherine Applegate
> - *Love, Ruby Lavender* by Deborah Wiles
> - *Poppy* by Avi
> - *Something to Hold* by Katherine Schlick Noe
> - *The True Confessions of Charlotte Doyle* by Avi

FIGURE 7.1 *Our class chart of adjectives*

brave	loyal	humble	optimistic
courageous	determined	radiant	pessimistic
strong	persistent	amazing	joyful
funny	wise	kind	creative
rude	wicked	selfless	beautiful
selfish	smart	helpful	vain
loving	intelligent	friendly	
caring	timid	despicable	
adventurous	shy	naughty	

"Wow! We have quite a list of words up here. When we describe a character with an adjective, we call it a *character trait*. So if we think Ereth is funny, then *funny* is a character trait for Ereth. One of you said Sophie was shy, so *shy* is a character trait for Sophie."

✳ Day Two: Exploring Character in a New Mentor Text

Today I will read a new book to my students: called *Wangari's Trees of Peace* by Jeanette Winter. It is a true story. The real person and title character, Wangari Maathai, is very strong. Lots of evidence in the text support several character traits, so I decide this book will work well as a mentor text, even though it is not fiction.

After reading the book to students, we stop to talk about many elements of story, but we really focus on character. I ask students, "What adjectives would you use to describe Wangari? What are some character traits for her?"

Julien answers, "She's brave."

"She is really determined," adds Jayger.

Joseph says, "She's smart."

I record students' ideas on our chart. (See Figure 7.2; you'll find a template of this form on page 137.)

FIGURE 7.2 *Students' ideas for describing character are recorded on a chart.*

Wangari Maathai	
Character Trait	**Evidence From the text**
brave	
determined	
smart	

I now go back and help students to analyze their thinking. I point out to students that there are three ways we learn about characters:

- By what they do (actions).
- By what they say or think.
- By what others say about them.

I write this on a chart; see Figure 7.3. "So what evidence from the text do we have to support that Wangari is brave? What does she do or say? What does she think? What do others say about her?"

Drew says, "She keeps planting the trees even though they were putting her in jail and threatening her."

"She went far away from her family to go to school. That's brave," adds Jessica.

I add both of these ideas to our chart under "Evidence From the Text."

"Okay," I continue, "What evidence do we have that Wangari is determined?"

Isabella says, "She gets all those women to help her."

"And she didn't give up. She had to keep planting and planting. She knew it would take a long time to get all the trees back," says Alex.

Again, I add this to our chart. "And what evidence do we have that proves Wangari is smart?"

Jane says, "She got a scholarship to go to school in America."

"Yes. She must have been smart," I add.

"And she thought of the idea to plant the trees and pay the women to help her," says Cole.

Our updated chart is in Figure 7.4.

FIGURE 7.3 *Class chart*

Teaching Tip

Charting ideas helps focus students' thinking.

FIGURE 7.4 *Students' ideas continue to be recorded on the class chart.*

Wangari Maathai	
Character Trait	Evidence From the text
brave	She keeps planting trees even though they put her in jail and threatened her. She went far away from her family to go to school.
determined	She gets the women to help her. She keeps planting and planting, even though she knows it will take a long time, she doesn't give up.
smart	She gets a scholarship to go to school in America. She thinks of the idea to replant the trees and pay the women to help.

I close this lesson by saying, "Tomorrow we will use our chart of traits and evidence to plan a new, different kind of writing."

Day Three: Prewriting for a Literary Essay—Modeled Writing

I review with students the importance of writing about what we read. "You know that one of your choices in Reader's Workshop is *Writing About Reading*. Your reader's notebooks are filled with great thinking about the books we have read together and the books you have read on your own or in small groups. You have made predictions, recorded inferences, asked questions, and discussed new facts you have learned. You also have written down interesting language you have come across and connections you have made between books and your own lives. Today I am going to model a specific kind of writing called a literary essay. A literary essay is a writing piece about an aspect of literature."

I continue, "A literary essay can focus on one element of a story, like plot, setting, theme, or character. Today, we are going to focus on *character*. Like other kinds of writing, a literary essay has several paragraphs. It needs a lead or opening paragraph. This is where the writer introduces the book and in this case, the character. The middle paragraph or paragraphs tell about the character, sometimes starting with a little background—how old, whether he or she is human or a kind of animal, what happens to the character at the beginning and middle of the story. Then the writer describes the character and provides evidence for what he or she is saying about the character. The ending paragraph or conclusion will wrap things up and maybe tell how this character changed or how he or she affected the reader/writer."

To model, I share a graphic organizer that will help me plan my essay. I review our chart with the character traits for Wangari and text evidence (see Figure 7.4). I use this information as I complete my graphic organizer, thinking aloud as I record ideas. See the complete graphic organizer in Figure 7.5. You'll find a blank template of the organizer on page 138.

FIGURE 7.5 *Teacher-modeled plan for an essay*

Wangari Maathai

Lead: Introduce the character and book.

Wangari Maathai—real woman from Africa who changed the world.

Book by Jeanette Winter

Body or Middle: Give background about the character and story. Discuss two character traits and provide evidence.

She is a woman living in Kenya who goes to school in America and comes back to find the trees are being cut down in her country.

Brave—She stands up to the men. She plants trees even though they put her in jail.

Determined—Gets women to plant trees. Keeps planting even though it is dangerous. Keeps planting even though it will take a long time to replace the trees that were cut down.

Smart—She gets a scholarship to college in America. She thinks of this idea to replant the trees. She pays women to help her.

Conclusion: Why is the character strong and unforgettable? How did he or she change and/or affect other people?

She started out as a young, naive girl and ended up making big changes for her country and the world. She won the Nobel Peace Prize. She inspires me to do something good.

✳ Day Four: Drafting a Literary Essay—Modeled Writing

I gather students and begin my lesson. "Today I am going to write my draft of a character analysis essay about Wangari Maathai. During the last two days you helped me come up with some great character traits for Wangari, and then I was able to plan out my writing on this chart [see Figure 7.5 on page 75]. I will use the chart to help me organize my paragraphs."

I continue, "First, I will begin with my lead paragraph. I want to hook my reader or, in other words, grab my reader's attention. I think I will mention the book my character comes from and give a brief introduction."

I think aloud as I write my first few sentences.

Good books have interesting characters. In the book *Wangari's Trees of Peace*, the main character, Wangari Maathai, is very strong. She is actually a real woman from Africa who changed the world.

I reread my paragraph aloud and ask students some questions. *Did I introduce my character? Did I tell the book title? Did I say at least one sentence about my character?* Students agree that I did. Now I am ready to begin the middle, or body, of my paper. Again, I think aloud as I write. "I need to start with some background information about Wangari and the story."

Wangari was born in Kenya. She grew up with lovely trees around her and took them for granted thinking they would always be there. She loves her country, but she does so well in school that she earns a scholarship to study in America. When she comes back to Kenya, she notices many of the trees have been cut down. Kenya looks different, and she decides to do something about it.

"I will continue with the body or middle of my paper. I want to talk about how smart Wangari is but I think I will change the word *smart* to *intelligent*. I need to give information from the story to support that she is intelligent." I write in front of students, supporting my idea that Wangari is intelligent. I refer to my character trait chart and the column with the evidence from the text.

Wangari is very intelligent. She thinks of a plan to plant little seedlings to replace the trees, but she is just one woman. She gets other women to plant trees, too, and she thinks of the idea to pay them if the seedlings stay alive.

"Now I am ready to tell that Wangari was determined and brave. I think I will put these in the same paragraph." I think aloud about the government men who hit Wangari with clubs and the men who put her in jail. But she kept planting. I write again in front of students, thinking aloud with questions like *What did the government men say? What did they do to her?*, and *What did she do?*

Some people don't like what Wangari is doing. They say, "Women can't do this," but Wangari is determined and brave. She keeps planting. The government men hit her with clubs, but she keeps planting. They put her in jail, but she keeps planting. And she inspires a whole nation of women to keep planting.

 10 Essential Writing Lessons © 2013 by Megan Sloan, Scholastic Teaching Resources

I reread my two first paragraphs and then decide I am ready for my conclusion, or final paragraph. "Okay, now I must pull this all together. I need to tell what Wangari's achievements mean to me. How has her story affected me or changed my life?" I think aloud in front of students and then begin to write my conclusion.

Wangari shows us that you can do anything you set your mind to do. She started out as a naive girl, but she ended up changing the world. She inspired others, and she stood up for what she knew was right. At the end of this story, Kenya had green trees again. Wangari Maathai won the Nobel Peace Prize for her work, and she made the world better by being who she was. She inspires me to be a better person and to do something good, too.

I reread my piece again to make sure it sounds the way I want it to sound and says what I want it to say. I revised and edited as I drafted, but I read one more time to check for any corrections in spelling, capital letters, and punctuation marks. I review the organization of my essay, going though the following parts.

- *Lead*: Introduce the character and book.
- *Body or Middle*: Give background about the character and story. Discuss two character traits and provide evidence
- *Conclusion*: Why is the character strong and unforgettable? How did he or she change as the story progressed and/or affect other people?

My final draft appears in Figure 7.6.

FIGURE 7.6 *Complete character essay*

> Good books have interesting characters. In the book *Wangari's Trees of Peace*, the main character, Wangari Maathai, is very strong. She is is actually a real woman from Africa who changed the world.
>
> Wangari was born in Kenya. She grew up with lovely trees around her. She loves her country but she does so well in school that she earns a scholarship to go to school in America. When she comes back to Kenya she notices many of the trees have been cut down. Kenya looks different and she decides to make a change.
>
> Wangari is very intelligent. She thinks of a plan to plant little seedlings to replace the trees, but she is just one woman. She gets other women to plant trees too and she thinks of the idea to pay them if the seedlings stay alive.
>
> Some people don't like what Wangari is doing. They say, "Women can't do this" but Wangari is determined and brave. She keeps planting. The government men hit her with clubs, but she keeps planting. They put her in jail., but she keeps planting. And she inspires a whole nation of women to keep planting.
>
> Wangari shows us that you can do anything you set your mind to do. She inspired others and she stood up to people for what she knew was right. At the end of this story, Kenya has green trees again.
>
> Wangari Maathai won the Nobel Peace Prize for her work and she made the world better by being who she was. She inspires me to be a better person and to do something good too.

I conclude by saying, "Sometimes characters do not inspire you or affect you in a strong way like Wangari, but remember, you are choosing to write about favorite or unforgettable characters, so they will probably be strong in some way. Tomorrow we will write a plan for a character essay we will write together."

✳ Day Five: Brainstorming Character Traits and Evidence From Text—Shared Writing

"Okay. Yesterday I wrote a literary essay about Wangari Maathai. Today, we are going to brainstorm some character traits for a favorite character in one of the books we are reading now." We are almost finished with our read-aloud *Mrs. Frisby and the Rats of NIMH*, so I suggest we write an essay about the main character, Mrs. Frisby.

We begin by thinking of character traits for Mrs. Frisby. Students brainstorm the following: *selfless, courageous/brave, determined,* and *caring*.

I record these traits on the lefthand column of our chart, then ask students, "What proof can we state to support these traits are accurate for Mrs. Frisby? Let's start with *selfless*. I really like that word. What does Mrs. Frisby do, say, or think that supports she is selfless? Or, what does another character say about her that supports this trait?"

Taylor says, "She helps Jeremy even though it is dangerous and she could have been eaten by the cat."

"Great point! Let me record that on the righthand column of our chart."

We continue with the three remaining traits on our chart and record ideas from the text to support them; see Figure 7.7.

FIGURE 7.7 *Students record evidence from the text to support the character traits they identify.*

Mrs. Frisby	
Character Trait	**Evidence From the text** *What does she say, think, or do? What do others say about her?*
selfless	• She helps Jeremy even though it is dangerous and she could have been eaten by the cat. • She went to see the owl for Timothy's sake. • She volunteered to put the powder in Dragon's bowl for Timothy.
courageous/brave	• She went to see the owl even though it was dangerous. He could have eaten her. • She went to see the rats. • She volunteered to put the powder in Dragon's bowl.

10 Essential Writing Lessons © 2013 by Megan Sloan, Scholastic Teaching Resources

determined	• She doesn't give up. She goes to the owl for advice. • She goes to the rats for help.
caring	• She takes care of her children and worries about Timothy. • She goes a long way to get medicine for Timothy.

"Wow, look at our chart! We have some great character traits for Mrs. Frisby, as well as evidence from the text to support them. Tomorrow we will make a plan for our essay about Mrs. Frisby."

✳ Day Six: Planning a Literary Essay: Shared Writing

I begin our lesson by reviewing our chart of character traits and evidence from the text to support these traits. "Now we are ready to make our plan for our essay. Let's look at the graphic organizer I used for Wangari."

I review the structure of our essay (see page 137). Using this structure, we begin to fill in our organizer; see Figure 7.8.

FIGURE 7.8 *Shared student plan for essay*

Lead or Opening: Introduce the character and book:

Mrs. Frisby and the Rats of NIMH by Robert O'Brien

Mrs. Frisby is strong. The book is fantasy. She persuades other characters to help her.

Middle or Body: Give background about the character and story. Discuss two character traits and provide evidence.

Timothy is sick. Mrs. Frisby must find a way to move her house. Who will help her?

Selfless—she puts others before herself (Timothy, rats, going to see the owl)

Courageous—she goes to see the owl and the rats. She flies on the crow's back. She volunteers to put the powder in Dragon's bowl.

Conclusion: Why is the character strong and unforgettable? How did he or she change and/or affect other people?

She makes us think things are not always hopeless. Her family is most important to her.

We reread our plan, and I tell students, "Tomorrow we will use our plan to write a draft of our character essay about Mrs. Frisby, just like I did with Wangari."

✳ Day Seven: Drafting a Literary Essay: Shared Writing

Our lesson begins with our planning chart in front of us. Next to it, we have our blank chart paper. "Today we will write our character essay about Mrs. Frisby. We will use our plan to help organize our paragraphs. We need to begin with a solid lead sentence. Our opening paragraph needs to introduce our character and our book. Let's think of a good first sentence."

Jenna says, "Mrs. Frisby is only a mouse, but she is a very strong character."

"Okay." I record her thinking. "Now, let's talk about the book."

Ryan says, "She is the main character in *Mrs. Frisby and the Rats of NIMH*."

"Shall we talk about her problem?"

Vivan says, "She has a big problem and has to go though a lot of scary situations to solve it."

Our lead paragraph reads:

> Mrs. Frisby is only a mouse, but she is a very strong character. She is the main character in *Mrs. Frisby and the Rats of NIMH*. She has a big problem and has to go though a lot of scary situations to solve it.

"Okay. Let's let that sit for now and move on to the body, or middle, of our paper and our next paragraph. In this paragraph, we need to give a little more background about Mrs. Frisby and the story." We reread the similar paragraph I wrote about Wangari, just to get ideas for organization. Then we look at our planning chart for specifics. Students offer ideas, and I record, asking questions along the way.

> The story starts with Mrs. Frisby's son, Timothy, being very sick. Mrs. Frisby will have to get medicine, but that won't be enough. Moving Day is coming, and Timothy will die if he is out in the cold too long. Mrs. Frisby has to ask for help from an owl and some rats she doesn't even know. She is scared at first, but gains confidence with each new character she meets.

We reread our paragraph; then we continue, drafting paragraphs for each trait and a conclusion. When we finish, I reread the entire piece. I suggest, "I think it is a good idea to let our writing sit for a day. Tomorrow let's come back and make some revisions and edit any places that need to be fixed."

Teaching Tip

Let your writing sit for a day and come back to revise and edit.

✳ Day Eight: Revising and Publishing a Literary Essay: Shared Writing

We are now ready to revise our piece and make editing changes. Students reread the piece on their own and write down any suggestions they have for revision. Then we read our essay together, and students begin to make suggestions.

Immediately, Roman says, "I think we should say *encounter* instead of *go through* when we are talking about the scary situations. I also think we should change *scared* to *frightened*." The class agrees, and we make these changes.

We keep reading, considering suggestions, and making changes, even adding a new sentence at the end. When we finish, we reread the essay and are pleased with the changes; see Figure 7.9.

FIGURE 7.9 *Revised character essay*

Mrs. Frisby is only a mouse, but she is a very strong character. She is the main character in Mrs. Frisby and the Rats of NIMH.

She has a big problem and has to encounter a lot of scary situations to solve it.

The story starts with Mrs. Frisby's son, Timothy, being very sick. Mrs. Frisby will have to get medicine, but that won't be enough. Moving Day is coming, and Timothy will die if he is out in the cold too long. Mrs. Frisby has to ask for help from an owl and some rats she doesn't even know. She is frightened at first, but she gains confidence with each new character she meets.

Mrs. Frisby cares for her four children and is especially worried about Timothy. In the beginning of the story, it is obvious she is selfless when she helps a crow get untangled from the fence, even when she is in danger of being eaten by the cat. She puts her children first and her love for her children gives her courage. Mrs. Frisby travels a long way across cat territory to get medicine for her son. She goes to see the owl, even though he could have eaten her. And she goes to the rats for help, knowing they don't like to be bothered. Everyone knows to stay away from the rats. Her determination keeps her going, and she does not give up, even when things seem impossible.

In the end, Mrs. Frisby's problem is solved, and she ends up making some new friends and feels different about the rats she used to stay away from. Her experiences make her more confident. It is clear her family is important. She makes us feel like with a little courage and determination, problems can be solved. Everything is not hopeless, even though it seems like it.

Shared-to-Independent Writing: Prewrite for Essay

Now it is time for students to choose a character as the focus of their individual literary essays. I invite students to look closely at the books around the room. Carrying their writer's notebooks allows students to jot down the names of their favorite characters from the books they have read. Students may also borrow ideas from our class chart of characters and traits.

Students share the characters they write down in their notebooks. We talk briefly about each one, brainstorming some adjectives or character traits that match them. I ask students to choose one character to focus on and caution them, "Make sure this is a character you can describe with two or three strong words."

✳ Day Nine: Prewriting for a Literary Essay— Independent Writing

Today students are given a graphic organizer to glue into their notebooks. They will complete the character traits and evidence columns either alone or with a partner. I find letting students work with others gives them opportunities to talk about the characters, their traits, and evidence from the text that will support their ideas. This talk time is so important before students write. It allows them to process their thinking.

I stop by Maddy. She is rereading *Sophie and Lou* by Petra Mathers, a class favorite from earlier this year. I sit down next to her and ask, "How are you doing?" Maddy shows me her character trait chart. "I see you have a couple of traits written down with some evidence," I say. "Tell me what you wrote first."

Maddy says, "She is determined."

"What evidence from the story do you have to support this?"

Maddy answers, "She wanted to learn how to dance so bad she painted the floor."

"What do you mean?" I ask.

"Well, she painted the different steps for the dances in different colors."

"Okay. What else do you have?"

Maddy answers, "She is shy. She always goes to the store during the lull hours."

"What does that mean?"

"It means when no one is there. That way she doesn't have to talk to anyone."

"That makes sense. It looks like you are still working to add another trait. You are off to a great start." See Maddy's prewriting in Figure 7.10.

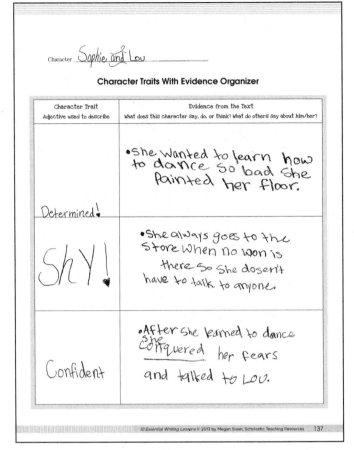

FIGURE 7.10 *Maddy's Trait Chart*

✳ Day Ten: Planning a Literary Essay—Independent Writing

I tell students, "Today, you are going to take your traits and evidence organizer and use it to help you make a plan for your essay." I hand out the Literary Essay Graphic Organizer: Character, which students will eventually glue into their notebooks (you'll find a template on page 138). We discuss the planning boxes for each part of their essay. "You will need an opening paragraph to introduce your character and the book. Then you will need a middle or

10 Essential Writing Lessons © 2013 by Megan Sloan, Scholastic Teaching Resources

body. This section might be one, two, or three paragraphs. Here is where you will talk a little more about the story and also include your character traits and evidence. Finally, you will need a concluding paragraph where you tell about why this is an important or unforgettable character."

Students begin writing in their plans for their essays. They include ideas from their character traits/evidence pages. I go back and revisit Maddy. She begins to transfer some of the information from her character trait chart onto the plan for her essay. She has added *confident* as a third character trait. I ask, "Now, how can Sofie be shy and confident?"

Maddy answers, "Well, she is shy at the beginning of the story, but she loves dancing so much that she becomes confident by the end of the story."

"Oh. So she changed over the course of the book?"

Maddy answers, "Yes."

I leave her to complete her plan for writing; see Figure 7.11.

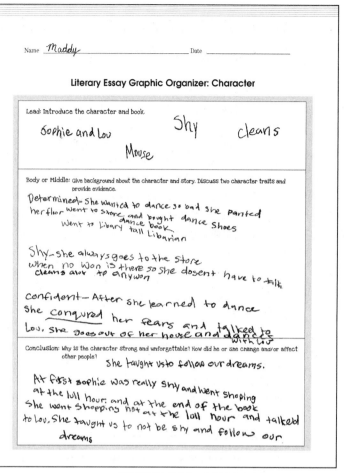

FIGURE 7.11 *Maddy's planning sheet*

✳ Day Eleven: Drafting a Literary Essay— Independent Writing

Today is the day students will use their plans to write their first drafts. I encourage students to take one paragraph at a time. "Begin with your lead. Remember, you need to introduce your character and your book." We review my lead paragraph about Wangari Maathai as well as our shared lead paragraph about Mrs. Frisby. Both continue to hang in the classroom, serving as mentor paragraphs for students.

Dylan begins his lead paragraph. He is a little stumped, so I encourage him to look at what he wrote on his plan.

> Poppy is a strong character. She is a mouse. *Poppy* is the book. She has to solve the family's problem of needing to move.

> ### Teaching Tip
>
> Encourage students to "borrow" ideas for lead sentences, transitions, and ending sentences from both your modeled piece and the shared-writing piece when writing their own essays.

I begin conferring with Dylan. "Okay. It looks like you have some good ideas in your introduction box. How might you begin? Let's look how we began for Mrs. Frisby." We read what we wrote:

> Mrs. Frisby is only a mouse, but she is a very strong character. She is the main character in Mrs. Frisby and the Rats of NIMH.
> She has a big problem and has to encounter a lot of scary situations to solve it.

"How can you start without just copying what we wrote about Mrs. Frisby?"

Dylan says, "Poppy is the main character in the book *Poppy*."

"Great. Write that down. Now, what next?"

Dylan and I have a conversation about Poppy being strong and how she has a big problem, just like Mrs. Frisby, and it even has to do with moving, just like Mrs. Frisby. But there are differences.

Dylan writes:

> Poppy is the main character in the book *Poppy* by Avi. She is a strong character who has a problem. She must go up against Mr. Ocax (the owl) to find a solution for her family.

I praise Dylan for his first paragraph and encourage him to reread it several times and maybe even find a partner to listen to it, until he feels it is right. I leave Dylan to do some independent work, but will come back to check on him when he begins his second paragraph.

Teacher-Student Conferences With Student Share

I continue to meet with students around the room. I gather students and have a couple of them share their first paragraphs so other students can gain inspiration.

Maddy shares her first paragraph about Sophie in *Sophie and Lou*.

> Sophie is the main character of the book *Sophie and Lou*. Sophie is a mouse that is really shy. At the beginning of the book, Sophie likes to clean her house. It is always spotless. Sophie always goes to the store at the lull hours so she doesn't have to speak. She also puts her head down when she sees people on the street.

> ### Teaching Tip
>
> Have a couple of students share their beginning paragraph to help inspire (and give ideas) to other students.

Ryan also shares his first paragraph.

> Mr. Ocax is not a very likeable character. In fact, you don't like him at all. He is the villain in the book *Poppy*. I like to celebrate the villains in books because they really make stories interesting.

We discuss Maddy's and Ryan's first paragraphs and talk about the fact that they are short. "They both introduce their characters, and Maddy actually begins to tell us what her character is like at the beginning of the story. Ryan is waiting until his second paragraph to tell more about his character."

Conference with Maddy

I follow Maddy and ask her about her plans for paragraph two. She shows me her plan and feels confident about what she wants to write. I meet with another student, and when I come back, Maddy reads to me her second paragraph.

> But everything changes when the dance studio gets built across the street. She gets determined to learn how to dance.

I stop Maddy here. "I love that first sentence. You move to your second paragraph with a very smooth transition: *But everything changes when . . .* It makes me want to read on. Let me ask you something else. What is it that gets Sophie determined?"

Maddy answers, "The music."

I suggest Maddy revise and add that in. She rewrites: *When she hears the music she gets determined to learn how to dance.*

Maddy continues reading her paragraph:

> Sophie goes to the library and checks out a book on how to dance, even though she is afraid of the librarian. Sophie also paints her floor different colors for different dances.

Here I ask, "What are some of the dances she is learning?"

Maddy says, "The fox-trot and the samba."

"Would you like to add those as examples so your reader will get an idea of the names of the dances Sophie is learning?"

Maddy agrees and adds *like the fox-trot and samba.*

I ask Maddy to read me the first sentence of her next paragraph.

> Sophie becomes confident.

This gives me a perfect opportunity to talk about transitions again. "What made her become confident?"

Maddy answers, "As she learned to dance."

"That is wonderful. Could you include that somehow before you talk about her becoming confident?" Maddy tries it out.

> As Sophie learns to dance, she becomes confident.

"That is lovely. Perfect!"

Maddy reads on, and I continue to ask questions to help her revise for details and clarity. I remind her that she has already used the words *At the beginning of the story and As Sophie learns to dance* to highlight some of Sophie's character traits. I suggest she might want to use words like *At the end . . .* or *By the time she meets Lou . . .* so we can see what Sophie is like when the story comes to a close. Her final essay appears in Figure 7.12 on page 86.

FIGURE 7.12 *Maddy's essay*

Sophie is the main character of the book *Sophie and Lou*. Sophie is a mouse that is really shy. At the beginning of the book Sophie likes to clean her house. It is always spotless. Sophie always goes to the store at the lull hours so she doesn't have to speak. She also puts her head down when she sees people on the street.

But everything changes when the dance studio gets built across the street. When she hears the music she gets determined to learn how to dance. Sophie goes to the library and checks out a book on how to dance even though she is afraid of the librarian. Sophie also paints her floor different colors for the different dances, like the fox-trot and samba.

As Sophie learns to dance she becomes confident. She goes to the shoe store to get new shoes and on the way home she actually smiles at Lou. At the end of the book she conquered her fears and talked to Lou. Sophie taught us to never give up and follow what you love to do.

Sophie also taught us not to be shy. Sophie became confident and learned that she doesn't need to be shy and also learned to dance. She also found out that learning something new can be a good thing and can really open up your heart.

Maddy Shares With the Class

Because I feel there is such power in students sharing their drafts, I gather students again and have Maddy share her essay on the document camera. She explains her revisions, and students can see where she has crossed out some words and added some. I direct focus to her transition phrases.

> At the beginning
> But everything changes
> As Sophie learns to dance
> At the end

I ask Maddy if she would highlight those so students can really see them. Students ask questions and now have another mentor text, or model, for their essays as they continue to write and revise their drafts.

Student-teacher conference

✳ Final Thoughts

In this chapter we tackled character essays. The same process outlined here can be used to teach literary essays focused on setting, theme, or plot. Start with several great mentor texts so students can analyze the literary element; then model how to plan and draft an essay. Gradually release responsibility to students, and when they feel successful—and only then— have them choose a book in which they will analyze the literary element independently.

Writing an Informative Article

Students love to read expository text. They devour the books and magazines in the nonfiction section of my classroom library. Books about animals, people, places, jobs, and of course, world record books, are often found in the hands and book boxes of my students, especially the boys. Small groups of kids crowd around a book or magazine filled with interesting information. They point. They stop to talk. They share ideas and ask questions. Nonfiction texts elicit talk.

I encourage students to read both fiction and nonfiction texts. It is important that, in addition to the imaginary stories so popular with my students, they read informational text, including books, magazines, newspaper articles, maps, directions, and more. It is important for me to read aloud good nonfiction texts.

Students reading nonfiction

✳ Day One: Exploring Expository Text

I begin our unit on writing expository text by asking each student to find a nonfiction text in the classroom. I give students time to explore the shelves and choose a book, magazine, or chart. We come together and share our finds. Students share *ZooBooks, Sports Illustrated for Kids, Scholastic News*, books about zebras, ponds, recycling, Harriet Tubman, Walt Disney, Washington State, and more. After everyone has shared, I ask, "What do you notice about these nonfiction or expository texts?" Students agree they all give information. Then I ask, "What types of text do we have here? I notice some of you brought books about people. What are those books called?"

Several students answer, "Biography."

"Right. Some of you have books about animals, places, and sports. What else do we have? Oh, I see Jenna has an Ed Emberley drawing book. That gives information about how to draw different animals. Let's see what it looks like inside." Jenna holds up the book for people to see the step-by-step pictures. "And Domenic, you have something different. Hold that up. What did Domenic pick?"

Ryan says, "A magazine."

"Yes. Magazines are filled with informative articles. Who else has a magazine?"

Margaret raises her hand and holds up her *ZooBook* for us to see again.

I now ask, "What do you notice about the special text features we see in nonfiction/expository text? We have been studying about this. Some of these features are sometimes included in fiction text, but mostly we see them in nonfiction."

Students begin to rattle off some of the text features we have discussed up to this point: maps, diagrams, captions, bold print, and more. I ask students to see if they can find examples of text features in the books or magazines on their lap. We share with each other. Julia notices, "I have a map in my book, but there is also a map at the beginning of *Poppy* and that's fiction."

Katie adds, "And there's a map at the beginning of *Love, Ruby Lavender*, too."

"You are right. Why do you think those fiction authors placed a map in their stories?"

Julia answers, "So we can follow where the story is taking place?"

"Yes. Kind of for the same reason nonfiction authors include them. So we can see where the real stories they are telling are happening."

As we talk about author's purpose, types of expository text, and special text features, I record our thinking on a chart, such as the one shown in Figure 8.1.

Teaching Tip

Let students explore nonfiction articles and other text before writing this text type.

FIGURE 8.1 *Our class chart on expository writing*

Expository Writing

Purpose	Types	Special Text Features
• to inform or give information	• informative article • biography • how-to • report • directions • recipes	• bold print • labels • captions • table of contents • index • diagrams • maps • tables • photographs/ illustrations • headings • pronunciation keys

For our remaining time today, I encourage students to read an expository or nonfiction text with a partner or by themselves. I tell them that tomorrow we will be learning more specifically about one of these types of text.

✳ Day Two: Sharing Mentor Texts

I want students to narrow their thinking today and focus on one type of expository text: an informative article. I ask, "Where do we usually find articles?"

Tyler says, "In magazines."

Jayla adds, "And in newspapers."

"Right," I respond. "And what is the purpose of an article?"

Cheyenne answers, "To give us information."

"Yes. To inform us."

There are many resources you can visit to find short appropriate articles to use as mentor texts. Some of these are *Scholastic News, Time for Kids,* or other student magazines like *ZooBooks* or *Sports Illustrated for Kids.* In addition, I can find short articles in our literature anthology and local newspaper.

I choose to share an article from *Scholastic News* (March 19, 2012, Edition 4). The article is entitled "School on a Bus." I chose this article because it is current, interesting to students, and short. The entire article fits on one page and is five short paragraphs.

> ### Resources for Informative Articles
>
> - *Time for Kids*
> - *Scholastic News*
> - *Sports Illustrated for Kids*
> - *Kids Discover*
> - *ZooBooks*
> - literature anthologies
> - *National Geographic for Kids*

I display the article under the document camera and gather students close so we can first look at what is there. I read the title, "School on a Bus" and then ask students, "What do you notice? What text features pop out at you?"

Jenna says, "There are two photographs."

"Do these help you in any way?" I ask.

Trent answers, "Yes. They kind of show us what it looks like. The seats are around the edge of the bus and they all have little chalk boards.

Kyle adds, "And they decorated the outside of the bus."

"Yes. I notice it says, 'School on Wh . . .' What do you think the rest of that word says?"

Ryan says, "School on Wheels."

"I bet you are right. Okay, what else do you notice before we begin reading?"

"There is a map. I think this is happening in India because it is the only country in green," says Jeremy."

"Okay. So we know this is about school on a bus and it probably is happening in India. Does anyone have a question?"

Jayger asks, "Why do they have school on a bus?"

Jared replies, "Maybe they are poor like the kids in Pakistan, and they don't have a school."

"Good thinking," I say. "Any other text features you notice?"

Albina says, "Oh. There is a word in bold print, and it has a pronunciation key. It's *poverty*."

"What do you think *poverty* means?" Surprisingly, students have some ideas, but none knows the exact definition. Then Jayger sees there is a definition. She reads, "It means *the state of being poor*."

"Yes. That is what *poverty* means. Now this is making sense, isn't it? Here is an article about kids going to school on a bus. They may not have a school because they are too poor. Are you ready to read?"

I read the article aloud a first time, discussing the content, asking questions, referring to the map and the photographs. Then I ask students to examine the article with a different eye. "What makes this an informative article? We already noticed that it includes lots of text features: a map, bold print, photographs, a pronunciation key, and a caption. But so do nonfiction books. Turn and talk about what makes this an article."

Students talk with a partner, and when we come back together, I ask the question again. "What makes this an informative article besides the text features we mentioned earlier?"

Melody says, "It has information."

"You are right. It tells us information about a school that is on a bus. It tells details about why this bus is a school and where in the world this is happening. The writer actually *explains* why the school is on the bus. *Explaining* is a very important part of an article. What else?"

Ryan adds, "It is in a newspaper, kind of."

"Yes. Our *Scholastic News* is a small newspaper. Where else do we find articles?"

"In magazines," says Tom.

"This article is also short," I comment. "Most articles are not very long. And most articles are written by reporters. They are reporting on interesting topics or on things that are currently happening."

We end our lesson recording our observations about articles on a chart for reference later on; see chart in Figure 8.2.

FIGURE 8.2 *Our class chart on informative articles*

What We Notice About Informative Articles

- They report information.
- They are about real things, places, people.
- They explain ideas (giving more information about why).
- They are usually in magazines or newspapers.
- They are shorter than books (several paragraphs).
- They sometimes have nonfiction text features, like maps, bold print, or pronunciation keys.

---

* Day Three: Prewriting an Informative Article— Modeled and Independent Writing

Today I model for students a prewrite activity that will help them discover topics for writing an informative article. I tell students that the topics I consider for my article must be ones I know a lot about. I must be an expert on these topics because I will not be doing any research.

"Let's begin by assuming this big chart is a page from my writer's notebook." At the top of my page I write *My Expert List*. "I actually listed some ideas earlier in the year when we brainstormed 'Good Topics for Me' so if I get stuck, I can turn back and see what I wrote before."

I begin by making categories:

- Places
- Sports
- People
- Jobs/Hobbies
- Miscellaneous

Now I begin to tell students about some of my expert topics and record my ideas as I share. "Well, I grew up in Hawaii, so that's a place I know a lot about. I will also add our school under *places*. And I go walking down by the marsh in Kirkland, so I can add that place, too."

I continue, "I was a gymnast, so I will write that under *Sports*. And I will write down my nieces, Julia and Katie under *People*. I can also write down Harriet Tubman under *People* because I have read many books about her over the years and have learned a lot about her."

FIGURE 8.3 *My expert list*

I continue sharing and recording until I have several "expert" topics; see my chart in Figure 8.3.

Students Write Their Expert List

I now ask students to consider their expert topics. "What do you know a lot about or consider yourself to be an expert on?" Students make a chart in their writer's notebooks and record the categories I wrote on my chart. I encourage them to share with a partner. Then students go to work recording some of their expert topics.

During this time I walk around and meet briefly with students, helping them think of ideas. I meet with Maia. She is thinking. I say, "Maia, I notice you wrote your baby sister, Jane, under *People*. I just thought of something else we are both experts on. I know about big families, and so do you!"

She smiles and asks, "Where could I write that?"

I answer, "I don't think it really matters. It might be in its own category or maybe it comes under *People*. I think it makes a great expert topic, though."

I find Dylan having a hard time thinking of ideas. I ask, "What do you know about more than anything else? What have you learned about this year that you've been so excited about?"

Dylan answers, "Spiders."

"Yes. That is a great expert topic for you." Dylan writes *spiders* under a new category: *Animals.*

When students have their lists, I invite them to share with small groups of three or four, and then some students share with the whole group. I advise students, "Be thinking about which topic you would like to write about this week. Make sure it is a topic you know a lot of factual information about. Remember, this topic will be the focus of an informative article, not a story."

✳ Day Four: Planning an Informative Article— Modeled Writing

Today I will model for students how to choose one of their expert topics and write an informative article about it. I go back to my list and consider my topics. "Hmmm. I have a lot of topics I know about. Today I am going to pick one to write about. This is hard because I have a few I would like to choose. I think I will pick Hawaii. I grew up there, so I know a lot about Hawaii. Maybe I should turn to a new page in my notebook and record some ideas." See my brainstorming list in Figure 8.4.

I remind students that my purpose is to inform my reader and explain my ideas, so I am going to write this piece as though my reader has never been to Hawaii. "How many of you have never been to Hawaii?" Most students raise their hands. "Okay. Then I am writing this for you."

I continue to think aloud. "One of the things we noticed in the article 'School on a Bus' is that an informative article has a lead or introductory paragraph or few sentences. This is where the writer introduces the reader to the topic. Then there is a middle or body of the paper that includes information. This is the place for writing new ideas. Last, there is a closing paragraph or few sentences. This is called a conclusion. Here, the writer sums up the information and lets the reader know the article is at its end."

> ### Hawaii
> - beautiful beaches
> - palm trees
> - trade winds
> - friendly people

FIGURE 8.4 *Planning for my article*

Reviewing Mentor Texts for Leads

I continue my planning by thinking about the lead. I review several of our mentor texts for ideas, thinking aloud for students as I consider ways to begin my piece. "In our mentor article I noticed the writer tried to get the attention of the reader in an interesting way. She made a bold statement, 'For millions of kids in India, getting an education is a big challenge.' Then she followed that sentence with 'But in some parts of the South Asian country, school buses have come to the rescue. The buses don't take kids to school, though. The buses are the schools.' Immediately, I have questions and think, *That's odd. The buses are the schools?* Her first paragraph got me interested to read on. How many of you thought the same thing? Now let's look at some others to get more ideas on how to begin an expository piece." I share the following leads to illustrate some common ways of opening an expository piece.

Starting with a strong factual statement:

"On August 24 in the year 79, people in the Italian city of Pompeii (pom-**pay**) were startled when a nearby mountain began to rumble."

— *Scholastic News*: "Blast From the Past," Jan. 2, 2012, Edition 3

Starting with a question:

"Have you ever needed to buddy up with someone to solve a problem?"

— *Scholastic News*: "Team Time," Sept. 5, 2011, Edition 3

"How do you picture a dinosaur? Does it have feathers? Fossil feathers found in pieces of amber are providing new information about what dinosaurs looked like."

— *Time for Kids*: "Dino Feathers," Sept. 30, 2011, Edition 3–4

> **Teaching Tip**
>
> Explore leads of articles to gain ideas for writing an opening sentence or paragraph.

Makes-you-think statement:

"It was not a trick, though it felt like one to many kids in the Northeast."

— *Time for Kids*: "Next Stop: Mars," Nov. 11, 2011, Edition 5–6

We discuss different strategies the writers use to get our attention. These include starting with a question, using a bold statement, including a big statistic or fact, or a statement that just makes us think or ask our own question.

Planning the Lead Sentence, Body, and Conclusion

I begin by making a plan in my writer's notebook. "I like the idea of starting with a question. I think I will try that." I display the Planning Graphic Organizer: Informative Article (see p. 139) for all to see and record ideas in my introduction box. Then, I

FIGURE 8.5 *My plan for my informative article about Hawaii*

Name _____

Remembered Time _____

Planning Graphic Organizer: Informative Article

Introduction: Get the readers' attention
Have you ever been to Hawaii? There are lots of things to see and notice. It is different than the other states. Called paradise.

Topic 1
Beaches

Topic 2
Weather

Topic 3
People

Conclusion:
Isn't this a great place?

move to the topic boxes. Here I write down three of the ideas from my notes: *beaches, weather, people*. Last, I record a question in my conclusion box.

I tell students, "This is just a first plan at this point. I know things will change and I will add lots of details and explain things, but this will keep me organized when I am ready to write my first draft."

Drafting the Informative Article

I gather students close as I begin to compose my opening. I tell students, "Just like in my plan, I think I will begin with a question like one of our mentor articles did."

Teaching Tip

Making a plan will help students organize their writing.

> Have you ever been to Hawaii? If you have, you know what a real treat this place is. Some people call it paradise.

I then work to add a couple of more sentences to introduce my topic. I want to explain why Hawaii is special. I tell students that I don't want to give away lots of details yet, but I can mention some. In fact, I want to give a little hint about what my article is about.

> It is like no other state in our country. It is the only state made up of all islands. Warm air, beaches, and beautiful people will make you want to stay forever.

I tell students that I am happy with my opening for the moment. Now I am ready to write the body, where I will give more information. I use my plan for ideas and work to elaborate on each idea. I tell students, "The first paragraph of my body is going to be about the beaches. Everything I include must be about beaches. And I need to explain what the beaches are like."

> The beaches in Hawaii are lovely. The water is a blue-green color and it is really warm. You won't have a hard time diving in. The white sand is soft. It tickles your toes and is warm to the touch. Sometimes, though, the sun can make the sand so hot you can have a hard time walking on it. Many people along the beaches build sandcastles. Some just watch the water float in and out, and some enjoy all the water sports available: swimming, surfing, and parasailing. While many people like Waikiki beach on Oahu, Kailua beach (on the other side of the island) is also a favorite.

I stop to reread my paragraph and ask students if I stayed focused on beaches for this part. They agree that I did. Now I am ready to write a new paragraph about the weather.

> The weather is always warm. In the summer it is usually 80–90 degrees. In the winter it is usually in the 70s but it can get warmer than that. Sometimes it is cloudy or rainy on one side of the island and sunny on the other side. The islands often are divided by mountain ranges. You can either drive around the edge of an island or go through the tunnels cut through the mountains. Even though it is humid, trade winds help you stay cool.

Again, I reread my paragraph to see if it makes sense. Students need to see this process of rereading and questioning one's self as a writer so they won't be afraid when they try it. *Did I elaborate? Did I stay focused? Should I add something there? Should I take that out?*

Now I am ready for my paragraph about the people.

The people in Hawaii are lovely. They are friendly and kind. There are people from every background and of every color: Hawaiian, Chinese, Filipino, Japanese, Black, Portuguese, White, and more.

I am now ready for my conclusion. I look at my planning sheet to get me started.

Hawaii is such a wonderful place. The beaches and weather make visitors want to come all year long. The Hawaiian people make visitors want to come back. Wouldn't you like to go?

I reread my entire article aloud making small changes when something doesn't seem quite right (adding a detail, changing a sentence, editing for spelling or punctuation). I am pleased with my work and tell students that tomorrow they'll begin planning their own expository piece.

✳ Days Five and Six: Planning and Drafting an Informative Article—Independent Writing

Now it is time for students to revisit their expert topic lists. I encourage students to add to their list if they think of something new. I display my plan (Introduction/ Body/ Conclusion) for students to see, and they get ready to do the same in their writer's notebooks. Students choose a topic and begin to write down ideas. Again, I roam around the room looking for students who might need some assistance. This is my time to confer one-to-one. I encourage students to share their ideas with others. Again, I remind students that this plan should include information. See one student's plan in Figure 8.6.

Now students are ready to write. I say, "Let your plan guide you, but remember to elaborate. Stay focused in each paragraph. Remember, your first paragraph is introducing your topic. Your middle paragraphs are focused on one idea each with lots of details added. Your last paragraph is your conclusion. You might restate something important you said and let your reader know the article has come to an end without saying: *The End*." I circulate to confer with students who need some support. Let your students be your guide for how much time to allow. They may need two or three days to complete their drafts.

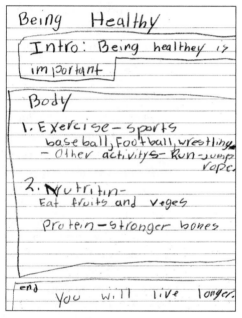

FIGURE 8.6 *Student plan for an informative article*

✳ Day Seven: Revising for Text Features—Modeled and Independent Writing

I gather students in front of our Expository Writing Chart (see Figure 8.1). I begin by saying, "You all worked really hard on your drafts of your articles the last couple of days. Now we are going to work to make them better by revising. We could focus on lots of different things, but I thought today we would focus our revisions on text features. Let's take a look at that part of the chart again."

10 Essential Writing Lessons © 2013 by Megan Sloan, Scholastic Teaching Resources

```
┌──────────────────────────────────────────────────────┐
│                   Text Features                        │
│                                                        │
│    •  bold print            •  maps                    │
│    •  labels                •  tables                  │
│    •  captions              •  photographs or illustrations │
│    •  table of contents     •  headings                │
│    •  index                 •  pronunciation keys      │
│    •  diagrams                                         │
└──────────────────────────────────────────────────────┘
```

We review the text features listed, and I suggest that some of these would not be appropriate for an article. For instance, a Table of Contents is used in books. Ryan adds, "So is an index."

"Yes. You are right. Let me read over my piece again and see if any of these text features might make sense."

After reading, I say, "I notice there are some interesting words that I could maybe put in bold print so they stand out as important. Words like *paradise, Waikiki, Kailua,* and *Oahu.* I know I shouldn't put too many words in bold print because then they won't stand out, so I need to choose wisely." I bold the words I chose. Then I note, "Another text feature that might be helpful is the pronunciation key. Some of these words are hard to pronounce so a key might help. What do you think?"

Students agree with me so I work to add pronunciation keys. Last, I consider adding headings to each of the paragraphs in my body. I can use the words I wrote in my plan: *Beaches, Weather, People.*

I add headings to see how they look, along with my title. My revised piece is shown in Figure 8.7.

FIGURE 8.7 *My revised informative article on Hawaii*

┌──┐
│   │
│   Hawaii   │
│   │
│   Have you ever been to Hawaii? If you have, you know what a real treat this place │
│ is. Some people call it **paradise**. It is like no other state in our country. It is the only │
│ state made up of all islands. Warm air, beaches, and beautiful people will make you │
│ want to stay forever.   │
│   │
│ **Beaches**   │
│   │
│ The beaches in Hawaii are lovely. The water is a blue-green color and it is really warm. │
│ You won't have a hard time diving in. The white sand is soft. It tickles your toes and │
│ is warm to the touch. Sometimes, though, the sun can make the sand so hot you can │
│ have a hard time walking on it. That has happened to me a few times. Many people │
│ along the beaches build sandcastles. Some just watch the water float in and out, and │
│ some enjoy all the water sports available: swimming, surfing, and parasailing. While │
│ many people like **Waikiki** (**Wi**-kee-kee) beach on **Oahu** (O-**Ah**-hu), some find it too │
│ crowded and like **Kailua** (Ki-**loo**-uh) beach on the other side of the island. │
│   │
│   *(continued on next page)* │
└──┘

Weather

The weather is always warm. In the summer it is usually 80–90 degrees. In the winter it is usually in the 70s but it can get warmer than that. Sometimes it is cloudy or rainy on one side of the island and sunny on the other side. The islands often are divided by mountain ranges. You can either drive around the outer edge of an island or go through the tunnels cut through the mountains. Even though it is humid, trade winds help you stay cool.

The People

The people in Hawaii are friendly and kind. There are people from every background and ethnicity: Hawaiian, Chinese, Filipino, Japanese, Black, Portuguese, White, and more. You will love the different cultures that bring interesting food to your plates, music to your ears, and customs you will adopt.

Hawaii is such a wonderful place. The beaches and weather make visitors want to come all year long. The Hawaiian people make visitors want to come back. When will you go?

Students Revise to Add Text Features

I encourage students to reread their drafts and look at the text-features chart. As they do, they should consider the following: *Which text features make sense to add? Do you have any words that are important? Maybe these need to be bolded. Do you have any words that might be hard to pronounce? If so, maybe I can help you with adding pronunciation keys. Do you want to add headings? Would a map be helpful or a photograph or drawing?* It's helpful to have students work in pairs so they can bounce ideas off each other.

While students are revising, I conduct conferences to help students in their decision making. I begin with Ryan who has written a piece about being healthy. I ask Ryan to read his article to me and to think if there are any really important words that might need to be bolded. We find the words *exercise* and *protein*. Ryan reads one part: *Really good eating is important.* I ask, "Ryan, what does *really good eating* mean? Is there another word you can think of that means exactly that?" Ryan is not sure, so I provide the word for him. "Have you ever heard the word *nutrition*?

Ryan answers, "Oh yeah."

"Would you like to use that word in your article?"

"Yes," he says, and he works to revise. Then I suggest that *nutrition* might be a good word to bold. I also suggest *vegetables* and *fruit*.

After reviewing, Ryan decides he would like to add headings. His revised piece is shown in Figure 8.8.

 10 Essential Writing Lessons © 2013 by Megan Sloan, Scholastic Teaching Resources

FIGURE 8.8 *Ryan's informative article on being healthy*

Being Healthy

If you want to live a long life, you need to have a healthy lifestyle. There are lots of things you can do to be healthy. If you do these things you have a better chance of living longer.

Good Nutrition

It is important to eat good foods like fruits and vegetables. Apples, oranges, grapes, broccoli, and carrots are all good foods that give you vitamins you need to stay healthy. You also need protein like meat and fish. Protein gives you energy. It is really important to eat something with protein in the morning.

Exercise

It is also important to exercise. It doesn't really matter what kind you do, just do it. Basketball, soccer, and gymnastics are fun ways to get exercise. You can get your heart rate up and have a good time. If you don't like sports, then you can walk at least or jump rope.

Keeping healthy is important. You can live to be 80 or 90 if you eat right and exercise. Just take control and do it!

✳ Day Eight: Editing and Publishing Informative Articles— Independent Writing

Students have a chance to share their drafts and revisions with each other, and I have a chance to confer with students about their changes. Now we need to decide how we want to publish these articles. Students decide to type them. First we go though our editing process. Students edit their own piece. Then they exchange articles with two other students for further editing. Last, they come to me or a parent helper, and together we make the last few changes for spelling, punctuation, indenting, and capital letters.

We are now ready to go to the computer lab. Students type their articles and print them. We make two copies: one for a class book of articles and one to take home. Students add illustrations, maps, or photographs, as needed, to complete their articles.

✳ Reviewing What We Learned

We review all we have learned over the last week and a half. Students share these ideas as I record:

- The purpose of expository text is *to inform*.
- Explaining is a big part of expository text.

- There are many types of expository text, including articles.
- Informative articles are written about topics we know about (expert topics). The information must be factual.
- Informative articles have a lead or opening paragraph, a body with one, two, or several paragraphs, and a concluding paragraph.
- Expository text often includes special text features.
- Writing informative articles is fun!

✳ Special Note About Shared Writing

It is always helpful to have a shared writing experience along with the modeled experience, or in lieu of the modeled writing experience if time is limited or you feel your students would benefit from active practice. Writing an informative article together, as a class, provides extra support before students work to write their own articles. Some ideas for shared expert topics are:

- Our School
- Important People in Our School
- Our Classroom
- A Recent Field Trip Destination
- A Classroom Activity like Writer's Workshop or Reader's Workshop
- Our School Principal
- A Letter to Future Students Coming Into This Grade Level

✳ Final Thoughts

Students love reading nonfiction. They love learning about real things. It makes sense that they might enjoy teaching others through writing. In this series of lessons we focused on informative articles. After reading, dissecting, and discussing what makes an informative article, I modeled writing an article about something I had some expert knowledge about. Students were then encouraged to choose a topic they already knew a lot about, organize their thoughts, and write a draft. It is important to note that research often goes along with writing an informative article. Sometimes we have a lot of knowledge about a topic but might need to search out some additional information. Coupling research with what the writer already knows about a topic can enhance the article and might make the information more reliable. I would encourage this kind of writing all year long, as students continue to ask questions about the world around them.

Writing an Opinion Piece

Everyone has opinions. Whether it is an opinion about an ice cream flavor, a call at last week's soccer game, or something more important—like which candidate would make the best president— most of us can render an opinion with the reasons we feel the way we do. Sometimes we stand firm in our opinions, and sometimes people argue against our stance and we change our minds.

As teachers we want students to develop opinions about lots of topics. We invite them to share opinions when we ask, "What do you think?" And then we ask them to back up their opinions with "Why do you think that?" or "How did you come to that conclusion?" In this chapter, we address opinion writing, exploring how to teach students strategies that will help them convey their opinions and support them with logical reasons, facts, and examples.

✳ Day One: Defining Opinion

While students have had practice distinguishing between fact and opinion in previous years, as well as during reading instruction this year, this group of lessons starts with a review of the terms so students are clear about what constitutes an opinion. I begin by asking students, "What is the difference between a fact and an opinion?"

Jared answers, "A fact is real. An opinion is something you think."

"Right. Does anyone want to add anything else?"

Ryan says, "A fact is definitely true. An opinion isn't."

I prod, "What do you mean by that? Can you tell me more?"

Ryan continues, "A fact is always true. It's been proven, like *cheetahs are the fastest land animals*."

"Okay. And an opinion?"

"An opinion is just something you think—like *cheetahs are cute animals*."

I add, "So everyone is going to agree with the fact: *cheetahs are the fastest land animal*, but maybe not everyone will agree with the opinion: *cheetahs are cute*. Some people might not think they are cute."

"Let's make a list of facts and a list of opinions." I make a T-chart (see Figure 9.1). "Does anyone have a statement you know is a fact?"

Jenny says, "Most cats have four legs."

"Does everyone agree that is a fact?"

Jada answers, "All cats have four legs."

Jenny responds, "No. My cat had an accident and only has three legs."

"Okay. So most cats have four legs." I record Jenny's idea on the chart. "Does anyone have an opinion about cats?"

Reece says, "Cats are adorable."

Again, I ask students if they agree that this is an opinion. I add, "My mom was scared of cats so she did not think cats were adorable. Even if a lot of people agree, it is only an opinion." We continue sharing facts and opinions and discussing each to make sure we all agree. We record our thinking in a chart; see Figure 9.1.

FIGURE 9.1 *Our chart categorizing facts and opinions*

Facts	Opinions
• Most cats have four legs. • Some snakes are poisonous. • Mt. Everest is the tallest mountain on earth. • The fifth graders sell popcorn on Tuesdays. • Joe Stoshak is a main character in the book *Honus and Me*. • In autumn, some leaves turn red, yellow, or orange before they fall from their trees. • Abraham Lincoln was our 16th president.	• Cats are adorable. • Snakes make good pets. • You have to be brave to climb Mt. Everest. • Popcorn should be sold twice a week. • *Honus and Me* is a great book. • Autumn is the most beautiful season. • Abraham Lincoln was our best president.

Our read-aloud book is perfect for thinking about and defining opinion. *There's an Owl in the Shower* by Jean Craighead George produces great conversation about the spotted owl/logger controversy. Students begin to see that there are often two sides to a story and have to figure out which opinion they will choose.

Independent Work With Fact and Opinion

I set students out to do their own fact/opinion work in their notebooks. "You can find facts in books and then think of a related opinion, kind of like what we did on our chart. Or, you can brainstorm some facts you know, along with opinions, with a partner and record them in your notebooks. After fifteen minutes, we will come back together and see what you came up with."

While students are working, I am able to check in on several groups and see how they are doing. After fifteen minutes, we gather back together and students share their facts and opinions.

✳ Day Two: Sharing Mentor Texts

When I think of opinion pieces, my first thought is of the editorial section in the newspaper. People love giving their opinions, and whether I agree with them or not, sometimes they are very informative, sometimes entertaining. While most newspaper or magazine articles have the purpose of informing their readers, sometimes writers have a definite opinion about the topic they are writing about. They may give their opinion or they might offer both sides of the issue and leave the decision or opinion up to the reader. Such is the case in the article I use with my students today. It is entitled "Rough Road Ahead" from our most recent *Scholastic News*.

I begin by saying, "Today we are going to read a short article titled 'Rough Road Ahead.' It actually gives us information about two sides of an issue. Let's read it first and then come back together and talk." I have students read the short article with a partner.

I begin the discussion with a question. "So, what is this article about?"

Ryan answers, "It's about the zebras and the wildebeests in Africa."

"Okay. What about the zebras and the wildebeests?"

Sofie answers, "They have to travel a long way to get food during different seasons."

Reece adds, "They migrate to grassy areas."

"Okay. So what's the problem?" I ask.

"People want to build a highway across the park where they travel," says Jenna.

I ask, "How is that a problem?"

"The cars could be dangerous for the animals and might make it too hard for them to get where they need to get," answers Ethan.

"I see. So they should just not build the road? Is that our opinion? Is there any reason we think they should build the road?"

Selina says, "The road would help the poor people there."

"How?"

Ryan says, "There aren't many roads, and the people can't get from one side of the country to another. It says (Ryan reads), *But Tanzania is one of the poorest countries in the world. It has few paved roads. Officials there say that the new highway would link eastern Tanzania with towns in the west, making it easier to transport and sell goods. That would help create jobs.*"

"Okay. We have some great thinking going on. Let's try to put this thinking on our chart. The question really is whether they should build the highway or not?" I make a T-chart with a heading for each side of the issue: *Build the Highway* and *Don't Build the Highway*; see Figure 9.2 on page 104 for our completed chart. I tell students, "What we have here is information to support two views or two opinions. One is to build the highway, and one is to not build the highway. Let's try to give reasons or support for each opinion and list them on each side of our chart." We discuss the various points and complete our chart, listing support for each side. We go over key vocabulary, like the word *hazards*, *migrate*, and *trek*.

FIGURE 9.2 *A T-chart helps us organize our thinking.*

Build the Highway	Don't Build the Highway
• It is a poor country, and the highway would help the people transport and sell their goods. • The highway would create jobs. • Connects the two sides of the country.	• Zebras and wildebeests already have a hard time surviving when they migrate (other animals like lions, crocodiles, and cheetahs track them). • The highway would cut them off from their grassy feeding areas. • The cars could create new hazards.

We review the two opinions the article presents and the support or reasons for each. I say to students, "Notice that the author actually included some facts to support each side. His arguments were logical and clear, and because he included facts, we listen with an open ear." I remind students, "This article introduces an issue and gives support for both sides. Sometimes people write opinion papers supporting only one side of an issue."

✳ Day Three: Charting Opinions About a New Mentor Text

Today I gather students to listen to the book *The Tale of Pale Male* by Jeanette Winter. It is a true story about a red-tailed hawk, nicknamed Pale Male, who has been mating and nesting in a skyscraper in New York City since 1993. I tell students, "As I read to you today, I want you to think about any opinions you begin to form in your mind."

Winter tells about the red-tailed hawk who, along with his mate Lola, builds a nest at the top of a skyscraper in New York City. Birdwatchers are fascinated, but the residents of the building do not like what comes along with a huge nest on their building (food scraps fall on balconies) and so they take the nest down. The bird lovers are outraged and form a protest. In the end, they make an agreement with the apartment owners, the nest is rebuilt, and it becomes home to many new chicks over the years. I read the book up to the part where they are deciding whether to let the nest be rebuilt. We study the wonderful illustrations and read a bit of the author's note at the end (just enough to not give away what happens—we will read the rest later).

I begin our discussion with a question. "So what do you think? Is there more than one opinion presented in this book?"

Julia answers, "The bird lovers want the nest to be rebuilt, and the apartment people want the nest to stay gone."

"Yes. They each have an opinion about this massive nest. What did the author say? Four hundred pounds of twigs, sticks, and bark? That's a big nest."

Reece says, "I think they should let the nest be rebuilt."

"Okay. Who else has the opinion to let the nest come back?" Most students raise their hands.

I continue, "But do the residents of the apartment building have a right to feel the way they do?"

Ethan says, "Yeah. I guess I wouldn't want to see lots of bones falling down when I look out my window."

Domenic adds, "Yeah. That was kind of gross."

"Okay. Why don't we make a chart like we did the other day?" Our T-chart lists both opinions at the top: *Rebuild the Nest* and *Get Rid of the Nest*. We discuss the reasons for each position and fill out the chart as shown in Figure 9.3.

We review our chart with the two opinions and support. I say, "Okay. Tomorrow we are going to choose one of these opinions and write a paper together, supporting our opinion." After a little discussion, students decide to write an opinion piece supporting *Rebuild the Nest*. I ask students to do some research in the classroom or at home to find out more about the red-tailed hawk—anything that would support our opinion to rebuild the nest. "One question we need to answer is: Are there many red-tailed hawks left or are they endangered?" Even though I know the answer to this, I want students to find out for themselves. A few students agree to research this question before tomorrow.

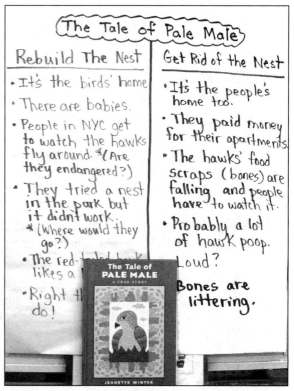

FIGURE 9.3 *Student chart*

✳ Day Four: Planning an Opinion Piece—Shared Writing

I begin by asking students what they found out with their research. Ryan brings a page he printed about the red-tailed hawk. "So, what did you find out?" I ask.

Ryan answers, "They aren't endangered."

"Well, while that is bad news for the purpose of the paper we are writing because that would have been a strong argument for keeping the nest, it's good news for the red-tailed hawk and birdwatchers who love them. Is there anything else you found interesting about the hawk that we might be able to use?"

Student share the results of the research, informing us that the red-tailed hawk is the most common hawk in North America and that they can do "spectacular aerial acrobatics" while mating. We decide that we have enough support to begin our planning, knowing that if we think of more we can always add it later.

Using a Planning Sheet to Plan Our Writing

After going over our support statements, I introduce our planning sheet to students; see

Figure 9.4 and the template on page 140. I say, "Just like all writing, we need an opening or lead paragraph that will introduce our topic and state our opinion. Then we need the body of our paper. This may include one, two, or three paragraphs where we will include logical reasons and facts to support our opinion. Then we will end with a concluding paragraph restating our opinion."

"Okay. Let's begin with a plan for our introduction or lead. There are different strategies we can try to make our first paragraph get our reader's attention. We studied some of these earlier this year when writing other genres. One way is to create a scene where you ask your reader to 'imagine' something—usually a bad thing that goes against your opinion. A second way is to start with a question. And a third way to start our paper is to begin with a bold statement or fact." Students recall our study of questions and bold statements in informative writing, and I see their nods of familiarity. I write these three lead ideas on a chart; see Figure 9.5.

"Let's try each of these leads and see if we have one we really like. Does anyone have an idea for creating a scene? We could use the word *imagine* and then add something that would not be a good thing. One of our statements of support is that this is the hawks' home. Maybe we can imagine someone taking our home away?"

Jared says, "Imagine building a home for your family, and one day you came back after school and someone had destroyed it, just taken it away."

I respond, "That's great. Let me write that down so we don't forget." I record Jared's idea.

"Okay. Let's try a question. Anyone have an idea?"

Maddy suggests, "Have you ever seen a red-tailed hawk do a trick in the sky?"

"All right." I record Maddy's question.

Jim says, "I have another question. 'Have you heard the story about Pale Male and Lola?'"

"Great." I add that to our chart. "Okay. How about a bold statement or fact?"

Ryan says, "Red-tailed hawks are the most common hawk in North America."

Again, I record Ryan's idea. Now comes decision time. "Which idea do you think would work best for our introduction or lead sentence? Turn and talk to one another for a moment."

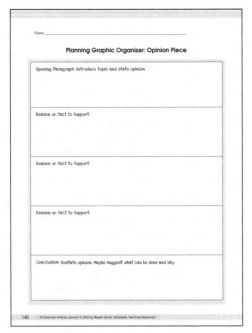

FIGURE 9.4 *Planning graphic organizer*

FIGURE 9.5 *Our chart on ideas for writing leads*

Teaching Tip

Record ideas for lead sentences/ paragraphs on class chart.

After some discussion, students decide on *Imagine building a home for your family, and one day you come back after school and someone has destroyed it, just taken it away?* I record this on our planning sheet in the opening paragraph; see Figure 9.6.

I remind students, "We can add to this later. This is just a quick idea, and we will elaborate when we actually write our lead paragraph."

Now it's time to focus on the body of our paper. Our planning sheet gives us room to record some of our best reasons to support our opinion.

After discussing our reasons, we realize some can be combined. For instance, *It's the birds' home* goes with *They tried to build a nest in Central Park but it didn't work*. And *People in New York get to watch* can be combined with *the hawks do spectacular tricks when they mate*. We record ideas in each of the boxes that will provide support for our opinion. Then I talk to students about order. "Sometimes when writers state reasons to support an opinion, they want to start with a strong reason, but they also want to end with their strongest reason for support. Which reason do you think is our strongest? Turn and talk to each other."

Students share ideas and decide that the fact that this is the hawks' home is the strongest reason, so we decide this will be our last reason stated.

"Okay. Now we are ready for our conclusion. Let's think of an idea, just a note, for what we want to say in our ending paragraph. Sometimes a writer will restate his or her opinion with an important idea."

Students decide on *We really believe they should let the nest be rebuilt for the sake of Pale Male and his mate*. Our finished planning sheet is shown in Figure 9.6.

FIGURE 9.6 *Our planning page for our opinion piece*

Rebuild the Nest

Opening paragraph: Introduce topic and state opinion.

Imagine building a home for your family, and one day you come back after school and someone has destroyed it, just taken it away . . .

Red-tailed hawks had nest taken down. They should be able to rebuild their nest.

Reason or Fact to Support:

New York City—Don't get to see birds like this very often (nature). Get to watch them do spectacular tricks when they mate. ("aerial acrobatics").

Reason or Fact to Support:

Red-tailed hawk is North America's most common hawk. We should take care of it.

Reason or Fact to Support:

This is the hawks' home. Babies have been born here. They tried to build a nest in Central Park but it didn't work. Where will they go?

Concluding Paragraph: Restate opinion. Maybe suggest what can be done and why.

Would you want your home disturbed? We really believe the nest should be rebuilt for the sake of Pale Male and his mate.

I remind students that this is just our plan. "We are going to use it to keep our writing organized but we may decide to change things around as we write." I add, "This is also just a skeleton of ideas. We will put a lot of muscle and skin on this by elaborating on our ideas."

✳ Day Five: Drafting an Opinion Piece—Shared Writing

The next day, we gather around our planning sheet and charts of ideas. We have a blank chart that we will use to begin our draft. After reviewing our plan and our notes, we are ready to begin.

"Let's begin with our opening paragraph. We decided to go with 'creating a scene' using the word, *imagine*."

> Imagine building a home for your family and one day you come back after school and someone has destroyed it, just taken it away.

"Does anyone have any ideas for how we can elaborate on this idea? I am wondering if we could talk about all the work put into building a home. I know Pale Male and Lola put in a lot of work building their nest because it was over 400 pounds of sticks and twigs and bark. What if we start out with *Imagine you built a home for your family* and add something right there? We could tell how long it took and how hard you worked."

Irvin suggests, "You worked on it for lots of months."

Reece adds, "It was hard work. You nailed all the boards and lifted a lot of heavy bricks."

"What are the bricks for?" I ask.

Julia answers, "The walkway."

I ask, "What else?"

Jenna says, "You painted all the rooms different colors and made them nice for your kids."

"Okay. How about the furniture?" I continue. "Did you have to move it into the house? And were you happy in your home?"

"Yes," answer Rashana and Elizabeth.

I record student ideas as they share. Then we go back to our original sentence: . . . *and one day you come back from school and someone has destroyed it, just taken it away*.

"We shouldn't start with *and*, so maybe we can make this the beginning of a new sentence."

Tyler suggests, "Then one day, you come back from school and someone has destroyed it."

I record Tyler's idea, and someone suggests we change the word *school* to *work*. Then Elizabeth says, "Why don't we say *destroyed your beautiful home*." Students agree and add, *It is all gone!*

We reread what we have so far, checking that it makes sense.

> Imagine you built a home for your family all by yourself. You worked very hard for months. You nailed all the boards and lifted heavy bricks for the walkway. You painted all the rooms different colors for your kids. You moved all the furniture in and you were happy there. Then one day, you come home after work and find someone has destroyed your beautiful home. It is all gone!

"Okay. Now we need to state what our paper is really about because it is not about you building a home. It's about one red-tailed hawk and his mate building a home. Sometimes when writers use this strategy of creating a scene, they then say *That's what happened* . . . Could

10 Essential Writing Lessons © 2013 by Megan Sloan, Scholastic Teaching Resources

we say that?" Students agree, and we craft the following sentences to end our first paragraph, stating our opinion.

That is what happened to two red-tailed hawks in New York City. They built a nest at the top of an apartment building, but some people didn't like it. The people took it down. We believe the red-tailed hawks should be able to rebuild their nest.

"All right," I say. "We opened with creating a scene. We told a little about the issue and we stated our opinion that the hawks should be able to rebuild their nest. What do you think? Are we ready to move to the body of our paper?" Students feel good about our opening paragraph.

I ask, "What is our first reason to support our opinion? Let's reread our plan."

Students begin a discussion, sharing their ideas. Jayger says, "If you live in New York City, you don't see lots of nature."

Rashana adds, "There are lots of buildings there, so it would be fun to see these birds in the sky."

Ethan adds, "And they do lots of cool tricks when they mate."

Ryan says, "And they are our most common hawk. We should take care of them."

I interrupt here. "Ryan, I notice we put that idea as our second reason, but I think we might like to start there and include it in our first paragraph. Should we try it out and see if we like it?"

Students continue to share as I record their thinking in our second paragraph.

The red-tailed hawk is the most common hawk in North America. It is a beautiful bird, and we should take care of it. New York City is a crowded place. There are so many buildings and not much nature. If the nest is rebuilt, the people who live there can enjoy the birds as they fly over.

At this point I prompt, "Can we elaborate here to tell what kinds of things the people will see as the birds fly over?"

Ethan says, "The spectacular tricks."

"Yes. In fact, you read to us the exact words that the author of the story used. What were they?"

Ethan reads, *"The spectacular aerial acrobatics."*

"We can use that if you want, as long as we put it in quotes." Students agree and we continue writing our paragraph.

While the hawks mate they do "spectacular aerial acrobatics." They dive and glide and do loop-de-loops like airplanes. That would be a sight to see!

I stop students again and ask, "Before we read about Pale Male, how many of you knew that the red-tailed hawk did those kinds of tricks while they mated?"

"I didn't," says Elizabeth.

"Do you think most people know this? Maybe we can turn our last statement into a question to make it more interesting. How could we do that?"

Taylor says, "We could say, *Did you know while red-tailed hawks mate, they do 'spectacular aerial acrobatics'?"*

We try that out. I revise by rephrasing that statement as the question Taylor suggested. It now reads:

> Did you know while red-tailed hawks mate, they do "spectacular aerial acrobatics"? They dive and glide and do loop-de-loops like airplanes. That would be a sight to see!

We are now ready to write our next paragraph. Again, we go back to our plan and review our notes. Students share ideas, and we draft paragraph two. I suggest a transition sentence (*Another reason to let the hawks rebuild their nest is . . .*) telling students that we need to remind our readers of our opinion that the hawks should be allowed to rebuild their nest. After discussion and drafting, our next paragraph starts like this:

> Another reason to let the hawks rebuild their nest is just common human kindness. Treat others the way you want to be treated. This is the hawks' home. They built it themselves. They tried to build it in Central Park, but it just didn't work for them. They need a high perch for their nest. This is where they want to have many more baby chicks.

At this point, I stop students and seize a teachable moment. I tell them that sometimes when you write an opinion, you bring up the opposite viewpoint to show your readers why that opinion is not as valid or appealing as yours. We discuss the fact that while this is the red-tailed hawks' home, it is also the home to people in the apartment building. They may not like the food scraps falling, so it may disturb their home to let the hawks rebuild the nest.

Students discuss ideas, and we add:

> We realize this building is also the home to many people and they may feel the hawks disturb them by dropping bones and other things they eat, but people are smart. We bet they can think of some solutions to this problem, and then everybody can be happy.

We reread our paragraph and decide we are ready to draft our conclusion. I remind students, "Our last paragraph needs to restate the topic and our opinion and end with a really strong statement." Again, students discuss ideas, and I record their sentences. After revisions, students write:

> We really believe Pale Male and his mate Lola should be able to rebuild their nest. This is a great opportunity for the people of New York to enjoy these beautiful North American birds as they soar above the skyscrapers. But more importantly, this is an opportunity to do the right thing. The hawks have chosen this apartment building in New York City to be their home. Welcome them back and let them rebuild their nest.

We reread our entire piece and make small revisions and edits.

After rereading our piece, I have students focus on our ending paragraph. "How many of you notice that as we stated our opinion in our last paragraph, we also tried to persuade or convince the people to let Pale Male and Lola rebuild their nest when we said, *Welcome them back and let them rebuild their nest*? Sometimes what starts out as an opinion turns into trying to persuade someone to agree with you. This is okay. This is really how many persuasive writing pieces begin. In our writing, we wanted to express our opinion, but we were so passionate about it that we wanted people to agree with us, too."

Now that we are finished with our opinion paper, we revisit *The Tale of Pale Male*. We read the last few pages, as well as the end of the author's note. Students are glad the people in New York let Pale Male and Lola rebuild their nest.

FIGURE 9.7 *Final shared draft of our opinion piece*

Let the Red-Tailed Hawks Rebuild Their Nest

Imagine you built a home for your family all by yourself. You worked very hard for months. You nailed all the boards and lifted heavy bricks for the walkway. You painted all the rooms different colors for your kids. You moved all the furniture in and you were happy there. Then one day, you come home after work and you find someone has destroyed your beautiful home. It is all gone!

That is what happened to two red-tailed hawks in New York City. They built a nest at the top of an apartment building and some people didn't like it. They took it down. We believe the red-tailed hawks should be able to rebuild their nest.

The red-tailed hawk is the most common hawk in North America. It is a beautiful bird. New York City is a crowded place. There are so many buildings and not much nature. If the nest is rebuilt the people who live there can enjoy the birds as they fly over. Did you know while red-tailed hawks mate they do "spectacular aerial acrobatics." They dive and glide and do loop-de-loops like airplanes. That would be a sight to see!

Another reason to let the hawks rebuild their nest is just common human kindness. Treat others the way you want to be treated. This is the hawks' home. They built it themselves. They tried to build it in Central Park but it just didn't work for them. They need a high perch for their nest. This is where they want to have many more baby chicks. We realize this building is also the home to many people and they may feel the hawks disturb them by dropping bones and other things they eat, but people are smart. We bet they can think of some solutions to this problem and then everybody can be happy.

We really believe Pale Male and his mate Lola should be able to rebuild their nest. This is a great opportunity for the people of New York to enjoy these beautiful North American birds as they soar above the skyscrapers. But more importantly, this is an opportunity to do the right thing. They have chosen this apartment building in New York City to be their home. Welcome them back and let them rebuild their nest.

✳ Day Six: Generating Ideas for Opinion Pieces— Independent Writing

Now it is time for students to write their own opinion pieces. I begin by reviewing the work we did together when we read the *Scholastic News* article and wrote our opinion piece about the red-tailed hawks in New York City. I gather students and say, "Now that we have had a chance to work together on writing an opinion piece, you will get a chance to write your own, using the same planning sheet we did."

Our first step is to generate some ideas or opinions. I share a couple of ideas to get them started. For instance:

- Dogs make great pets.
- Cats make great pets.
- Students should be able to chew gum in school.

I ask students to think about some opinions they have that might make a good topic for a piece of writing. They revisit some of the opinions they wrote in their notebooks the other day. They also work with partners to generate more, and then we come back together to share.

I write their ideas on chart paper; see Figure 9.8. When we are finished, I tell students that tomorrow they will be choosing one of these or another opinion statement for their writing. I encourage students to talk to their families and friends tonight for more ideas.

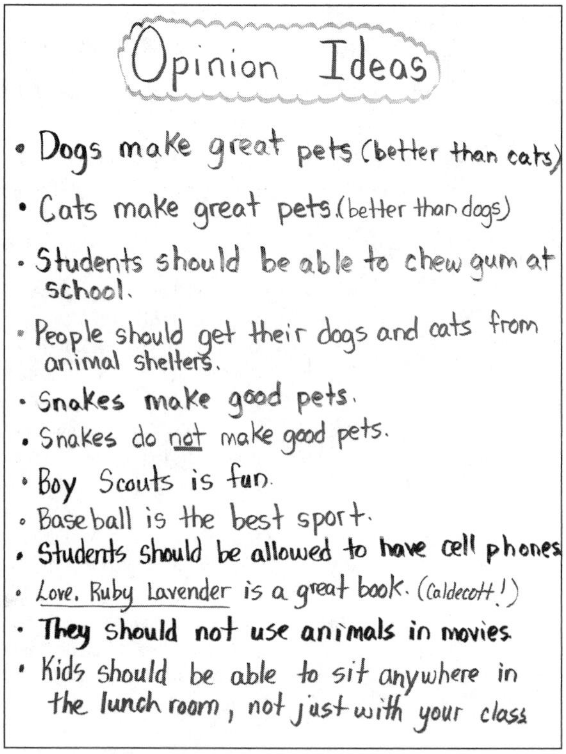

FIGURE 9.8 *Student-generated Opinion Ideas*

✳ Day Seven: Planning an Opinion Piece—Modeled and Independent Writing

When I gather students for our lesson today, I first ask if anyone has any additional opinion ideas.

Ryan says, "Kids should play soccer."

Maia adds, "It is fun being part of a big family."

Claire says, "The beach is a great place to go on vacation."

Other students share ideas, too. I encourage students, "You know, you can tweak some of these ideas for new opinions. For instance, I agree with Claire that the beach is a great place for a vacation. But I could also say, 'Camping is a great vacation.' Thanks, Claire, for helping me think of that new opinion idea."

I review with students the planning sheet we used for our shared opinion piece. I remind students they will be writing notes in the boxes and decide to guide them through part of this process. "Now that you all have your planning sheet, write your opinion at the top. You want to choose an opinion that you know you have some ideas to support."

Modeling: Opening Paragraph

I write an opinion on my chart (one I am sure no one has chosen). By writing my own plan in front of students, students have one more time to see how this is done. It provides support for students who are still unsure.

My opinion is: *People should walk every day*. I share, "I know I can try some different kinds of leads or opening lines. Let's look at our chart. I can start with creating a scene like we did with 'Let Them Rebuild the Nest,' or I can begin with a question. I can also begin with a strong fact or bold statement. You are going to have to make a choice just like I do. Hmm. I think I will try a question first. *Did you know that ___ people in America are overweight?* If I can find out that fact, I will have a strong question. Or I could just state that as a bold fact: *____ people in America are overweight*."

10 Essential Writing Lessons © 2013 by Megan Sloan, Scholastic Teaching Resources

I continue thinking aloud, "Or I could ask a question like, *Do you know how important it is to exercise?* And then I could say something about walking being a good way to exercise. I'm going to have to think about that. I am going to record these notes to help me remember my ideas."

When I finish writing, I say, "Now it is your turn. Think about how you might like to start." I give students some time to take some notes. I encourage them to share with a partner or even work with a partner to share ideas. While they do this, I walk around the room to confer with students.

Conference One With Tyler

I stop where Tyler is working. He is working on: *Camping is a good vacation.* I begin, "Tyler, I see that you have your opinion. By the way, I agree with you—camping is a good vacation. How do you want to begin your piece?"

Tyler answers, "I think I want to ask a question but I'm not sure how."

"Well, I know people have a hard time deciding on vacations sometimes. They might think of Disneyland, or going to the beach, or going camping. Maybe you could ask if people have ever had a difficult time deciding on a vacation. That's one idea."

Tyler says, "Have you ever had a hard time deciding where to go on vacation?"

"That's great. Then you could list some possible ideas. I gave you some examples, but you should think of your own. What are some other vacation ideas?"

Tyler says, "Sometimes we go to Great Wolf Lodge."

"That's one idea. How about another so you have at least two others besides camping?"

"We go to the beach sometimes."

"Okay. Do you want to list those so you don't forget when you are ready to write your paragraph?"

Tyler lists *Great Wolf Lodge* and *the beach.*

"Now you want to write down your opinion so you don't forget to add that later."

Tyler writes: *Camping is a good vacation.*

"I think you have some great notes for your first paragraph."

Conference One With Maia

At this point I move to Maia, who is writing an opinion piece about living in a big family.

I ask, "Okay. What is your opinion?"

Maia answers, "Having a big family is great."

"I really like that. You already know I am from a big family too, and I agree with your opinion. How did you decide to start?"

Maia reads to me from her notes: *Only child is not much fun.*

"Oh, I like that. Some people might think being an only child is fun. What do you say to that?"

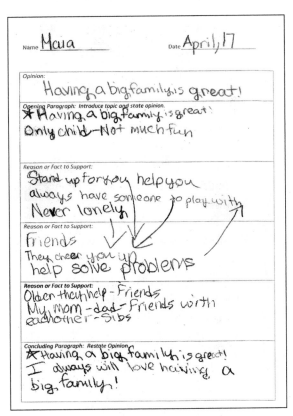

FIGURE 9.9 *Maia's planning page*

Maia smiles and says, "Being an only child might be fun sometimes, but you miss out." Then she reads more from her notes:

"When you are from a big family . . .

> *You always have someone to play with.*
> *You are never lonely.*
> *They stand up for you.*
> *They are your friends and help you solve problems.*
> *My mom and dad are still friends with their siblings.*

I respond, "Wow. You have some good notes that you really can elaborate on. I like how you remembered to write your opinion in your notes too."

Modeling: Body

At this point, many students have notes for their opening paragraphs. We now are ready to move to the body of our paper. I model with my chart.

I record three reasons in the three boxes of my planning sheet to support *People should walk every day.*

1. It is good exercise. Good for your heart. Helps you lose weight. Tell my experience walking.
2. You can do other things during walking—music, thinking, talking with a friend.
3. Makes you happy (endorphins).

I now encourage students to record notes to support their opinions. Again, I walk around the room, stopping for a few minutes to confer with individual students.

Conference Two With Tyler

I stop by to revisit Tyler. He already has his first reason down: *You get to enjoy nature.*

He seems to be stuck, not able to think of another reason. I ask, "Does camping cost much money?"

He answers, "Not as much as Great Wolf Lodge."

"That's right. A lot of people choose to camp because it a more affordable vacation," I comment.

Tyler adds: *It doesn't cost much money.*

I ask one more question. "Who do you camp with?"

"My mom and dad and my uncle and my cousins," says Tyler.

"So this gives you nice time to spend with family members?"

Tyler answers, "Yes. That's another reason I like camping."

I suggest, "Well, that could be your third reason. What do you think?" Tyler records his idea: *I get to spend time with my family.*

Tyler is on his way.

Modeling: Concluding Paragraph

After circling the room, I ask students to choose a partner and share their notes. I encourage students to help those who are stuck and may need another reason. When we gather, students are very excited, and I ask a couple of them to share with the whole class. Now students are serving as models for each other!

I say, "We are now ready to write just a couple of notes for your concluding paragraph." I model for students by writing on my own chart: *Do you want to stay healthy? Walking everyday is fun and great exercise.* I remind students that I am asking a question for my reader to think about and then I restate my opinion.

I ask students to work on notes for their conclusions, suggesting they work with a partner to help with ideas.

Tyler writes: *Camping is fun.*
It's a great vacation.

Maia writes: *Having a big family is great.*
I will always love having a big family.

Again, I encourage students to share with each other and help each other. This collaboration provides support for students who struggle to think of ideas completely on their own.

✳ Day Eight: Drafting an Opinion Piece—Modeled and Independent Writing

I tell students, "Today is the big day! You are going to take your notes and turn them into paragraphs, elaborating on ideas. Remember your notes are just notes. You have to add ideas so that you don't just have a list. You want to have sentences that flow together."

I begin modeling, turning my notes into an opening paragraph. I go back and reread aloud. "Hmm. I'm really still not sure how I want to begin. I will try though." As I write, I think aloud. I cross out things I don't like. I change things and add things as I go. I even change my opinion statement from *People should walk every day* to *I think walking is a great form of exercise.* Here's how my opening paragraph looks now:

> Teaching Tip
>
> It can be helpful to model writing a first paragraph, then have students try. Then model the next paragraph and have students try. Breaking the writing up like this will help make the task not seem so overwhelming.

> What if I could tell you about something you can do to add years to your life? It's easy and fun. It takes no money, and it will make you feel really good. It's no big secret. You just need a pair of legs. It's called walking. It's really good for you. I think walking is a great form of exercise.

I say, "Now it is your turn. Look at your notes. Try to write a few sentences. Remember to end with your opinion statement." I walk the room and confer with individuals as they begin.

Conference Three With Tyler

When I check in with Tyler, he is working on his paragraph.

I say, "I see you have written your question: *Have you ever had a hard time deciding where to go on vacation?* That is great. Read me your other ideas."

Tyler shares, *"Great Wolf Lodge, the beach."*

"Okay. So how will you add those ideas after your question? Could you somehow talk about the different choices families have when they decide on a vacation?"

Tyler writes:

> Have you ever had a hard time deciding where to go on vacation? You could choose Great Wolf Lodge or you could go to the beach, or you could even go to your grandma's house.

I continue working with Tyler. "It is great to say that these are also good vacation spots, but you want to make sure you give your opinion that camping is a really good—or maybe even your favorite—kind of vacation. Does that make sense?"

Tyler writes:

> Those are all good vacations. You will have a lot of fun. But I think the best vacation is camping, and I will tell you why.

I praise Tyler for his work and ask if he is willing to share his opening paragraph with his classmates to inspire them.

Conference Two With Maia

When I reach Maia, she is almost done with her draft of her opening paragraph. I ask her to read it to me.

> Imagine being an only child all alone. It doesn't sound very fun, does it? But how would you like having a big family? I love having a big family. They do many things for you.

I comment, "Wow. This is a great start. I like your first line and your details. There was one place I was feeling I wanted another detail though. Here, where you say *They do many things for you.* Are you going to go on to tell those things?"

Maia answers, "I think in the next paragraphs."

"Okay. I can't wait to see what else you write as you go onto the body of your paper."

While I want to guide students to elaborate and write for clarity and with detail, this is their piece of writing, so I want them to make the revision decisions, with my help. It is a real balancing act between teaching students and letting them own their writing.

My conference with Maia

Modeling: Body Paragraphs

Students continue working on their opening paragraphs. I encourage them to share with each

 10 Essential Writing Lessons © 2013 by Megan Sloan, Scholastic Teaching Resources

other and help each other with ideas. When I think most students have a first paragraph and are ready to move to the body of their papers, I gather students again and model once more.

"Okay. Now I'm ready to write my second paragraph. Let me look back at my notes." I reread aloud:

> It is good exercise.
> Good for your heart.
> Helps you lose weight.
> Tell my experience walking.

I begin to write, again showing students that this is difficult sometimes. Writers write something and then cross it out and start over. They reread over and over to see if the writing makes sense. I think aloud, *I like that. That doesn't sound right. I think I need to add something here.* Sharing what I am thinking as I write gives students a picture of what they should do as writers. It comes down to what Donald Graves said about the importance of modeling in front of students. "They need to see you struggle to match your intentions with the words that reach the page" (Graves, 1994, p. 110). This is how they learn to write.

I begin my second paragraph and immediately cross it out. I think aloud, "I am not liking this. I want to start over."

First Try:

Walking is easy. You can do it anywhere. I walk every day, and it makes me feel great. I know it is great for my heart.

Second Try:

Walking is great for your heart. It's an easy way to get your heart rate up, which is a good thing. My doctor says walkers live longer. Walking also helps get blood flow to areas that need some healing. I began to walk after I hurt my back. My physical therapist said walking would get lots of blood flow to my injured area and that would help with healing. And it did. Walking also helped me build muscle when I needed to shape up a bit.

Books That Help Foster Opinions

- *Fables* by Arnold Lobel (many of the fables foster opinions, especially "The Camel Dances")
- *The Librarian of Basra* by Jeanette Winter
- *Stone Fox* by John Reynolds Gardiner
- *The Tale of Pale Male* by Jeanette Winter
- *There's an Owl in the Shower* by Jean Craighead George
- *Who Is Melvin Bubble?* by Nick Bruel

Students Draft Independently

Students now work on the body of their papers. I talk individually with them as they work through the process of turning their notes into paragraphs. This drafting happens over the next couple of days. Students are encouraged to share with each other. Reading aloud to another student helps the writer hear his or her writing and may lead to revisions that will improve a piece.

At last, students work on their conclusion paragraphs. I model for students, and then they write. Again, I confer with students, asking questions and supporting them in turning their notes into great ending paragraphs.

FIGURE 9.10 *Maia's final opinion piece*

Maia April 18

Imagine being an only child all alone. It doesn't sound very fun does it?!? But how would you like having a big family! I love having a big family! They do many things for you!

One thing I like about having a big family is that they help you with homework, and problems you have. Sometimes when I need help with my homework my sister Avery helps me. And sometimes I help her with volleyball when she wants to practice. When you have a big family there is always someone there for you!

Another good thing about a big family is that you never are alone. You always have a playmate. They cheer you up when you're sad, they are always being a friend, and they stand up for you. It great having a big family!

Also a good thing about big families is that they always are your friends. Carter, Avery, Colby, and Jayne will be my friends forever. Just like my Mom and Dad are friends with their sibling still. I will always love having a big family.

✳ Final Thoughts

This unit of lessons has been a long process. By beginning with an article and studying what the writer does, students get a clear picture of what an opinion piece looks like. Sharing a picture book that helps students explore their opinion about a topic is a wonderful segue into shared writing; see some of my favorites in the box on page 117. Shared writing is such an important part of teaching students to write. It gives young writers a chance to write with the support and guidance of their teacher and peers. It also becomes a model for them as they begin their independent writing. Students apply what they have learned and feel confident to "give it a go."

Writing a Research Report

Children are curious about so many topics. My students come to me every day with questions about all types of things: *How many stars are in the sky? Why didn't Benjamin Franklin become president? What is it like to live in Afghanistan? How many home runs did Babe Ruth hit in his lifetime?* After studying about expository writing and composing their own informative articles about something they know (Lesson 8), students are ready to take on a larger project that involves research.

There are many possibilities for research topics; I list some of my favorites for grades 3–5 in the box below. Think about your science and social studies units. Consider students' interests in people and places in the world. Listen to the questions students ask and watch which nonfiction books they pull from the shelves to read. At some point, students will have full choice in their topics for research, but for now, we want to harness them a little, so we can really guide them through this process of research writing.

Possible Topics for Research

- The Planets
- Habitats
- Physics of Sound
- Plant Life
- The Human Body
- Compare Two Communities or Cultures

- People of History
- A Native American Tribe
- World War II
- Animals
- Sports
- Careers
- Weather

✳ Day One: Setting the Stage for Research

It is February, and my students are extremely interested in biographies. Because it is Black History Month as well as the month we celebrate President's Day, students are choosing to read books about Harriet Tubman, Jackie Robinson, and Abraham Lincoln, to name a few. I have lots of picture books about people in history: *Henry's Freedom Box* by Ellen Levine, *The Story of Ruby Bridges* by Robert Coles, and *Eleanor* by Barbara Cooney. I read these aloud, and they are very appealing to students. After reading a book, I usually ask, "Who would like to do more thinking about this person and this book?" The hands go up, and soon a full shelf of biographies becomes leaner. Student book boxes are filling up.

As we begin this unit, I review with students what makes a biography a biography. I remind them, "It is a kind of nonfiction, but it is its own genre. It is a book about a person who once lived or is still living." Since we have read many picture-book biographies up to this point in the year, as well as over the last week, my students are able to describe the kinds of features they notice in biographies. I set out several picture-book biographies for students to look at as we have this discussion.

I begin, "So what do you notice in general about biographies? I will record your ideas on this chart."

Richelle says, "They start when the person is born and end when the person dies."

"Yes. Besides maybe an introduction, most biographies begin with information about the person's birth and family. At the end, the author usually gives information about the person's death. What else?"

Jane says, "The author tells about the person's childhood first and then tells about the person as an adult."

"Okay. What else?" We continue discussing and charting students' ideas; see Figure 10.1 for our complete list.

FIGURE 10.1 *Student-generated chart on the characteristics of biography*

What Makes a Biography

- It's about a real person.
- It starts with information about a person's birth and family ends with the person's death.
- It tells the person's job or career.
- It is organized by time (starting with beginning of life, moving to adulthood, and then death).
- It sometimes includes quotes from the person or tells what other people said about the person.
- It sometimes includes a timeline.
- It sometimes has real photographs with captions.
- It tells what kind of impact this person has had on the world.

Day Two: Choosing a Person of History for a Shared Writing Piece

After a week or so of biography excitement, I gather students and read *Of Thee I Sing: A Letter to My Daughters* by Barack Obama. I love this book because it gives a snippet of several different Americans from Jackie Robinson to Sitting Bull, from Helen Keller to Billie Holiday. They are diverse in their backgrounds, ideals, careers, challenges, and nature. They all shine in their own ways, and students are excited to find out more.

I tell students, "President Obama's book is not really a biography. Instead, he introduces us to many Americans who are worth remembering. He gives us just a slice of information about each. He doesn't give us the whole pie." I am hoping students will become even more inspired to find out about one of these interesting people.

I begin, "Today, we are officially beginning our research about a person in history. You will each choose your own person soon, but before you do we are going to choose a person together, take notes using several sources (books, articles, etc.), and write our own short biography as a class. This shared writing will serve as a model for you when you begin your individual research paper."

> **Teaching Tip**
> Have students explore and describe the specific text type or form they will be writing after researching.

We discuss some options of historical figures to study. I want to make sure we have enough sources to read about this person, so I am very aware as students suggest and discuss these people in history. One of the people suggested is Helen Keller. Not only do I think she is an excellent person to study, but surprisingly not many of my students know much about her. I am also certain I have several sources we can use during our research and writing. So, I encourage this choice during our discussion, and students ultimately pick Helen Keller.

I start by asking, "What do you know about Helen Keller?" As I stated above, my students do not know much about this famous American. A few offered these comments:

- I think she was blind.
- She had a famous teacher but I forget her name.
- Her teacher helped her but it wasn't easy.
- I think she was deaf, too.

That was all students could offer. I smiled, knowing we chose the right person to study.

We begin reading a short chapter book titled *Who Was Helen Keller?* by Gare Thompson. I also grab all of the books about Helen Keller from our book baskets and set them out on a table. These include *A Picture Book of Helen Keller* by David Adler, *Helen Keller* by Stewart Graff and Polly Anne Graff, *Helen Keller: Courage in Darkness* by Emma Carlson Berne, *A Girl Named Helen Keller* by Margo Lundell and Irene Trivas, and several more. My texts are of varied reading levels so everyone can be involved. I encourage students to skim these over the next few days. I share with students that as we read, we are going to take notes. We are going to choose three main sources (books or articles) for information gathering so I will need their help with this when we are ready.

✳ Day Three: Beginning Our Notes—Shared Writing

Our next job is to come up with some guiding questions we want to answer, or ideas we want to explore through our research. Each topic of research has its own unique questions. With the study of a person of history, there are some predictable questions such as: *When was this person born? What was his/her childhood like? What did this person do for a living?* I encourage students to think about what they want to know about Helen Keller. I ask, "What questions do you have?"

Students come up with a list of questions, in no particular order:

- When/where was she born?
- What was her family like?
- What was her childhood like?
- What did she do for a living/career?
- Why is she a person we remember?
- What were her major accomplishments?
- What impact did she have on other people or the world?
- Does she have any famous quotes?
- Who was important in her life?
- Did she get married or have children?
- What important events happened in her life?
- Did she ever get to see?
- Did she go to school?

We have chosen our three sources for taking notes. They include our chapter book, *Who Was Helen Keller?* by Gare Thompson, *A Picture Book of Helen Keller* by David Adler, and an article from *Scholastic Printables*. I guide students to make these choices over others for specific reasons.

1. *Who Was Helen Keller?* is a chapter book and will be one kind of book most of my students will read when they choose a person to study. Its longer length gives us at least a week of reading time to think about Helen Keller's life and take notes on what is most important.

2. *A Picture Book of Helen Keller* is obviously an illustrated book. It also has a lot of great information about Helen Keller. We can move through the book slowly, and it still will not take a lot of time. Also there is a timeline in the back of the book.

3. "More Miracles for Helen Keller: An Unexpected Hero" is an article. This teaches students that sometimes your sources should represent a variety of genres. This short article can be printed for students and will provide practice using a highlighter or writing in the margins when searching for important information. Unlike the other two sources, each child will have a copy of this text.

I display an empty graphic organizer and suggest we fill it in with our most important questions; see Figure 10.2 (you'll find a reproducible version on page 141 in the appendix).

Since our research report is going to be three or four paragraphs, I make at least three charts and divide our questions to match each paragraph. This organizer will help students when we move from note-taking to writing the first draft of each paragraph. For instance, paragraph one will include information about birth, family, and childhood. Paragraph two and perhaps three will include information about the person's early adult life, middle adult life, career, and major accomplishments. The last paragraph will include information about the person's later life, impact on the world, death, and other interesting facts. First, we note our sources along the left column, then we record our questions at the top.

FIGURE 10.2 *Note-Taking Graphic Organizers for Paragraphs*

Note-Taking for Paragraph One

Questions/ Categories	When/where was Helen born? Family?	What was her childhood like?
SOURCE 1 *Who Was Helen Keller?* by Gare Thompson		
SOURCE 2 *A Picture Book of Helen Keller* by David Adler		
SOURCE 3 "More Miracles for Helen Keller: An Unexpected Hero" Scholastic Printables Article		

Note-Taking for Paragraph Two

Questions/ Categories	What did Helen do for a job or career?	What were her major accomplishments?
SOURCE 1 *Who Was Helen Keller?* by Gare Thompson		
SOURCE 2 *A Picture Book of Helen Keller* by David Adler		
SOURCE 3 "More Miracles for Helen Keller: An Unexpected Hero" Scholastic Printables Article		

Note-Taking for Paragraph Three

Questions/ Categories	Any famous quote by her or by Someone else about her?	Any other interesting facts? Impact on the world or other people's lives?
SOURCE 1 *Who Was Helen Keller?* by Gare Thompson		
SOURCE 2 *A Picture Book of Helen Keller* by David Adler		
SOURCE 3 "More Miracles for Helen Keller: An Unexpected Hero" Scholastic Printables Article		

Even though we are reading from *Who Was Helen Keller?* each day, for this lesson, I read our picture book biography. Students notice that sometimes the same ideas are in both texts. I remind them, "These authors also studied and researched, reading many sources before they wrote their own book or article." After reading *A Picture Book of Helen Keller*, students have ideas they want to record in our notes.

We talk about what note-taking should look like. I express to students, "We are not writing down complete sentences most of the time. We want words and phrases to help us remember our ideas. Sometimes note-takers use bullets to separate their ideas. We also don't want to copy sentences from any or our texts. We read and then we use our own words and maybe a few words from the book or article. The only time we copy something directly is when it is a direct quote. That means, something someone actually said. And then we put quotation marks around it. There is another time, too—when you are trying to spell a word correctly—then you may copy it directly from the book."

Students begin to share ideas for our notes. Some of these come from the beginning of *Who Was Helen Keller?* and some come from *A Picture Book of Helen Keller*. I record students' ideas.

✳ Day Four: Continuing Our Notes—Shared Writing

Again, we continue taking notes as we read our chapter book, but today I introduce a new source, our article titled "More Miracles for Helen Keller: An Unexpected Hero." I hand out the article to students and put them in pairs. I ask students to read the article and highlight any new or really important information that we might want to record in our notes. I remind students,

"When you use a highlighter, use it sparingly. Don't highlight everything or nothing will stand out. You have to decide what information is most important and most interesting."

Students read and highlight in pairs. I am able to circle the room and check in with each group. When they are finished, we discuss what students noticed.

Rashana says, "I like the beginning. The author used the word *Imagine* to begin."

I ask Rashana, "Can you read the first two sentences so we can all be reminded?"

Rashana reads: *Imagine the most famous person you know: Tiger Woods, Britney Spears, Prince William. Now think of this: Not one of them is as famous as Helen Keller was in her day.*

"That does grab my attention. We will have to remember how important the first couple of sentences are when we write our draft. What else do you notice?"

We continue with our discussion and begin adding notes to our chart next to our third source, the article.

As we continue reading about Helen Keller in our chapter book, *Who Was Helen Keller?*, we decide which ideas are important and/or interesting enough to include in our notes. We add to our chart when students feel they have learned something worth recording. Over a week's time, the boxes on our note-taking charts are filling up; see Figure 10.3. We now are ready to review our notes and begin our first draft.

FIGURE 10.3 *Student notes on Helen Keller*

Paragraph 1 Question or Category	When/Where was Helen born? Family?	What was her childhood like?	Paragraph 2 Questions or Category	What did Helen do for a job or career?	What were her major accomplishments?
Source 1 Who Was Helen Keller? by Gare Thompson	• Born June 27, 1880 Tuscumbia, AL. • Dad-Arthur - fought in Civil War, Called him "Captain." • Mom-Kate	• Healthy baby • Fever left her deaf + blind. • Parents let her be unruly. • Annie Sullivan came to be her teacher. • Learned sign language.	Source 1 Who Was Helen Keller? by Gare Thompson	• Author, Speaker • Ambassador for the Blind. • Actor - Vaudeville	• Learned to communicate. • First blind and deaf woman to graduate from college • Wrote books: *The World I Live In*, *Teacher* • Acted and spoke.
Source 2 A Picture Book of Helen Keller by David Adler	• Born June 27, 1880 • Mom and Dad loved her.	• Born healthy. Got a fever befor 2yrs old • Left her blind and deaf. • Played tricks. Locked mom in pantry. • Annie Sullivan - teacher • First words in sign lang. "water" • Went to School for Blind.	Source 2 A Picture Book of Helen Keller by David Adler	• Wrote books. • Visited with WWII soldiers who were injured.	• Graduated from college. • Wrote books: *The Story of My Life* • Won Presidential Medal of Freedom
Source 3 More Miracles for Helen: An Unexpected Hero (Article)	• Mom and Dad didn't think Annie could help.	• Spoke by grunting. • Wild and angry • Lonely (spent days in "dungeon of loneliness" she said. • Met Annie at 7yrs old • Learned to read and write Braille.	Source 3 "More Miracles for Helen Keller: An Unexpected Hero" Article	• Wrote books • Made speeches • Went to college.	• Learned to talk. • Learned to read and write Braille. • Wrote 13 books and hundreds of articles • Graduated with honors from Radcliffe. • Traveled around world.

✳ Day Five: Drafting and Revising Paragraph One— Shared Writing

It is now time to take our notes and begin to turn them into paragraphs. We begin with our notes for paragraph one. After reviewing them, I tell students, "Remember when Rashana noticed the first couple of sentences from our article. It said:

> Imagine the most famous person you know. Tiger Woods, Britney Spears, Prince William. Now think of this: Not one of them is as famous as Helen Keller was in her day.

"That is a strong lead. How many of you agree?" Students nod yes. "Let's read the leads from our other two sources." I read them aloud:

From *Who Was Helen Keller?*:
Helen Keller was born on June 27, 1880, in Tuscumbia, Alabama.

From *A Picture Book of Helen Keller*:
Helen Keller was born in Tuscumbia, Alabama on June 27, 1880.

I say, "The last two are very similar, and both of these seem to jump right in with information about when and where Helen was born. How should we begin our piece? We can start with an 'Imagine' statement or we can start with a bold statement. We can also just start with when and where she was born, although I don't think that is as interesting. What do you think?"

Elizabeth says, "I think we should say how brave she was."

Tyler adds, "We should say *Helen Keller was a very courageous woman*."

I ask the class, "What do you think? Do you want to start with this bold statement?"

Students agree to begin with this for now.

I say, "Okay. Now we probably want to tell the details about her birth."

Dianna says, "She was born June 27, 1880 in Alabama."

Tristin adds, "Her dad's name was Arthur Keller."

John says, "He fought in the Civil War. Everyone called him 'Captain.' "

As students share ideas, I record them. We continue with information about Helen's mom, and then students start telling about Helen and her illness. Melody says, "Helen was a smart baby."

"Then what happened?" I ask.

"She got a high fever," Jared answers.

I think aloud, "Okay. Helen was a smart baby but she got a high fever when?"

Jada answers, "Before she was two years old."

"Right. So how do we want to say this?" I ask.

After some discussion and revision students decide on: *Helen was a smart baby, but before she was two years old she became very ill with a high fever.*

I prod, "And then? What happened after that? Did she get well?"

Jason says, "She recovered, but the illness left Helen blind and deaf."

I ask, "How did her family feel about this?"

"They were sad," says Isabella.

"Just sad? How did they really feel? Remember, their healthy baby is now blind and deaf. How would you feel?"

Lisa says, "Her family was devastated."

 10 Essential Writing Lessons © 2013 by Megan Sloan, Scholastic Teaching Resources

"Oh, I love that word. That word really describes for me how I think they felt. Who agrees?"

We continue writing and revising: adding ideas, crossing out and changing things. Students sometimes remember something from the book that we did not include in our notes—some detail about a word or phrase. They look back and reread for the class, and we are able to add to our draft.

Our first paragraph now looks like this:

Helen Keller was a courageous woman. She was born June 27, 1880 in Tuscumbia, Alabama. Her dad's name was Arthur Keller. He fought in the Civil War. Everyone called him "Captain." Helen's mom's name was Kate. Helen was a smart baby, but before she was two years old she got a high fever. While she recovered, the illness left Helen blind and deaf. Her family was devastated. Helen loved the outdoors and loved playing tricks. Once she locked her mom in the pantry for three hours. But Helen was also unruly. She threw fits until she got what she wanted.

✳ Days Six–Eight: Drafting and Revising the Report— Shared Writing

I use the same process for drafting and revising paragraphs two through four. We consult our notes, discuss ideas, read and reread our writing. It is also the perfect time to talk about transitions.

When we reach paragraph four, I remind students that this is our last paragraph. It will focus on other interesting facts, famous quotes, and Helen's impact on the lives of others. Again, students share ideas. We revise and edit as we draft. Students decide what is important to include. They write about the people Helen met and include a quote about Louis Braille. They write about her passion for poetry and her favorite place to swim.

We reach the end, and I tell students, "Now we are at a very important part of our paper— the ending sentence or two. How does Helen have an impact on our lives? You know, I never met Helen Keller, but her story inspires me. If she could do all that she did with the challenges she had, then I should be able to do anything I set my mind to."

Sofie suggest, "Helen inspires us."

Maddy adds, "with her determination and courage."

I comment, "Lovely." I record their ideas. "What else should we add?"

Reece says, "She gives us hope and makes us believe things."

"What things?" I ask.

"She makes us believe we can get over anything," adds Brie.

I suggest, "You know, another way of saying that might be *She makes us believe we can overcome anything.*"

Brie says, "I like that better."

"Well, it means the same thing but maybe it sounds a little more sophisticated."

We have our two ending sentences now:

Helen Keller inspires us with her determination and courage. She gives us hope and makes us believe we can overcome anything.

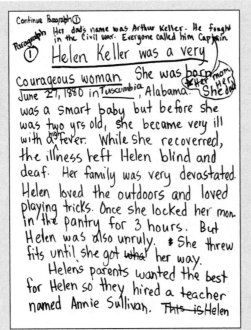

FIGURE 10.4 *Shared student draft with revisions*

"All right. Do we want to add one more sentence? Who thinks we need another bold statement to end our piece?"

Keven says, "Helen Keller was an amazing woman!"

"I think that is spectacular. Should we add that?" Students agree.

✳ Day Nine: Publishing Our Shared Research Report

Now is the time we type our paper. I have students take on this task. One student types at a time, as others volunteer to be editors. The page is projected onto our smart board. A group of students gather around for each paragraph and watch to make sure words are spelled correctly, new paragraphs are indented, and punctuation and capital letters are used correctly. (Teachers can take on the task of typing, too, but should continue to have student editors.)

After the paper is typed, we list our sources on a separate sheet of paper. Everyone receives a copy of our Helen Keller report. I use the margin to label what is expected in each paragraph. The annotated report will serve as a model for students as they begin their individual research report about an historical figure.

Teaching Tip

Keep shared-writing charts up as a reference for students as they work on independent research/note-taking.

Opening Sentence ↙

Helen Keller was a very courageous woman. She was born June 27, 1880 in Tuscumbia, Alabama. Her dad's name was Arthur Keller. He fought in the Civil War. Everyone called him "Captain." Helen's mom's name was Kate. Helen was a smart baby but before she was two years old she became very ill with a high fever. While she recovered, the illness left Helen blind and deaf. Her family was very devastated. Helen loved the outdoors and loved playing tricks. Once she locked her mom in the pantry for three hours. But Helen was also unruly. She threw fits until she got what she wanted.

Birth date place
Opening Sentence
Family
• Childhood

Helen's parents wanted the best for Helen so they hired a teacher named Annie Sullivan. Helen did not know that the day she met Annie would be the most important day of her life! Everything would change forever. Annie taught Helen to communicate using her hands to make words. This is called sign language. Her real breakthrough came when Helen learned to spell the word "water". Now Helen understood the signs she was making meant something. Finally, Helen went to a school for the Blind. Annie went with her.

Continued Childhood information

When Helen grew up she went to Radcliffe College. She learned there with Annie Sullivan. Helen was the first blind and deaf woman to graduate from College. She always loved writing and after school, she published two books, The *Story of My Life* and *The World I Live In*.

• Growing up
• Career
• Major Accomplishments

They were both best sellers and are still selling today. Later, she wrote the book *Teacher* about her beloved, Annie Sullivan. Helen was also a speaker, an actor on Vaudeville, and an Ambassador for the Blind. That means she raised awareness for the needs of blind people. Helen was so amazing to have learned to communicate with others, even with her handicap.

Career/ Major Accomplishments continued

Helen met some very famous people including 12 presidents, from Grover Cleveland to John F. Kennedy! She was also life-long friends with the great American author, Mark Twain. She met Alexander Graham Bell and Louis Braille. Helen said, "Louis Braille was a genius with God-like courage and a heart of gold." Helen had a passion for poetry. Her favorite place was Cape Cod, the place where she first swam in the ocean. Helen Keller inspires us with her determination and courage. She gives us hope and makes us believe we can overcome anything. Helen Keller was an amazing woman!

Ending sentence

• Other interesting information
• Famous quotes
• Impact on others

FIGURE 10.5 *Finished student research paper about Helen Keller*

✳ Students Begin Independent Research Projects

Now it's time for students to choose their own famous person to research and write about. Students have had plenty of time to skim the biographies in the classroom, and many have a book on hold in the library. I encourage students to choose a shorter chapter book from either the *Who Was?* series, *Time For Kids* series, or *History Maker Bios*. I also encourage them to find a picture book biography. In addition, students are allowed to look online for information from sources like *New World Encyclopedia*. I also have several *Scholastic Printables* articles ready for use.

There is a buzz around the room as students begin to gather their three sources and label their note-taking sheets with their name and the name of their famous person. Then they all settle in to read. I remind students that sometimes you need to read for a while and then stop to take some notes. "You cannot include everything. Your research paper will only be three to five paragraphs, so you want to take notes about the most important and interesting facts."

✳ Independent Reading and Researching

As students read and research each day, I am able to confer with individuals to see how they are doing. I meet with students and ask, "What can I do to help you?"

Sometimes the answer is "nothing." Some students have their research under control. Others will have questions like, "Do you think this is an important fact? Should I write it down?"

Always turn it back to the student: *What do you think? Is it interesting to you? Do you think it is important?* If the student isn't sure, suggest writing the fact down and say, "You can always cross it out later if it turns out it isn't really important."

Students also take their reading and research home each night. I expect them to work on this project at school and at home. Parents can support their children as they learn to paraphrase the words they are reading and record their ideas in their notes.

✳ Students Begin to Draft

Students will take a couple of weeks to read, research, and take notes about their famous person. When they are ready, it is time to begin the first drafts. I give students a drafting sheet to help keep them organized. It provides a line for the lead sentence of each paragraph. It also provides lots of space for the body and end of each paragraph. (See Figure 10.6 and page 142 for a reproducible template.)

I review for students the introductions or lead sentences we found in our three sources for Helen Keller. I encourage students to look in their three sources. Maybe one of the leads will inspire them. Most of all, I remind students, "You want your first one or two sentences to really stand out. Make it a bold statement or a question. Make it an 'Imagine' statement."

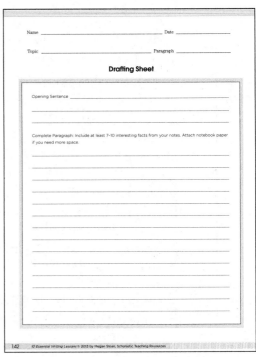

FIGURE 10.6 *Drafting sheet; see page 142*

 10 Essential Writing Lessons © 2013 by Megan Sloan, Scholastic Teaching Resources

Students Work on Leads

I confer with individuals who are working on their leads. Sometimes helping students get started with their opening sentence or sentences is the boost they need to keep going.

Conference With Drake

Drake is working hard to come up with a first sentence. He is unsure. I suggest we go back to some of the biographies in our classroom and look at how they started. I ask, "What do you notice?"

Drake says, "They tell what kind of person they are."

"Yes. Sometimes the sentence tells a special trait the person has. What words would you use to describe Walt Disney?"

"He is artistic."

I respond, "That is a great description of Walt Disney. How can you put that into a first sentence?"

Drake writes *Walt Disney was an artistic boy*.

I ask Drake, "What makes him artistic?"

He replies, "He invented all those characters like Mickey Mouse and Donald Duck. And he could draw really good."

"Those are some things you could add to that first sentence to elaborate."

Drake resists here. I sense he feels a bit overwhelmed so I suggest I be his secretary. I take out a sticky note and record what he said. Then I add, "Can you imagine a world without Walt Disney? What would be missing?"

Drake answers, "No Mickey Mouse. No Donald Duck. No Disneyland."

As I record Drake's ideas on the sticky note, I say, "Wow. It is pretty amazing to think about that, isn't it?"

Drake answers, "Yes."

I sense Drake really wants to move on to when and where Walt Disney was born. I give Drake the sticky note and suggest we come back together when he is ready and see if we he would like to use his notes to add more ideas to his first sentence, *Walt Disney was an artistic boy*. Even though Drake did not write his ideas down now, they are there for him later on the sticky note as he works to revise a lead that will catch the reader's attention.

Drake continues writing: *Walt Disney was born December 5, 1901 in Chicago*.

I say, "I think you are on your way. Now you can add information about his family and his childhood. Great start, Drake!"

FIGURE 10.7 *Drake's draft with revisions*

Students Continue Drafting

Drafting takes several days. I encourage students to draft one paragraph each day. I am there for help as they turn their notes into sentences for their paragraphs. I remind them, "You may do revisions as you write. You might want to cross out something or add something. You can use arrows and carets. This is your draft. Our draft about Helen Keller had lots of changes all over it. Remember that as you write your drafts."

Conference With Avery

I meet with Avery. She is writing about Anne Frank. I ask her, "How can I help you? What do you need from me to move forward?"

Avery says, "It is going to be hard to write all my paragraphs because Anne died when she was a child. She never was an adult and she never had a job or career."

"You are right. You are going to have to be flexible and creative in the way you organize your paragraphs. Anne never was an adult and she never had a career, but you know, they published her diary so she is a published author. Her diary is read around the world."

"I know," Avery answers.

"How about you think of dividing her childhood into two parts? Maybe your first paragraph can include her childhood before she went into hiding, and the second paragraph can tell about her time in the attic and also when she goes to the camp? Do you think that might work?"

Avery looks at her notes and says, "I think so. Maybe I could include when she first went into hiding in the first paragraph and then the later part of being in hiding in the second paragraph."

"That sounds like an even better idea." Avery now feels good about her plan, so I leave her to do her work.

Students Draft Conclusions

After several days, students have completed their drafts. The only thing left is drafting their ending sentences, which is so important, I dedicate a day to work just on it. Again, I confer with students individually, while also encouraging peers to work with each other.

Conference With Isabella

Isabella researched Barack Obama. She has most of her last paragraph and wanted help from me on the conclusion. She reads what she has and then says, "I want to tell all the things he has done in my last couple of sentences."

"Okay. What has he done? Let's review."

Isabella answers, "He was a senator. He is an author. He is the President, and he won the Nobel Peace Prize."

"All right. So let's think how you can say all of that so it sounds interesting. Maybe you can say something like *Barack Obama has accomplished a lot.*"

Isabella says, "I like that." She writes that down and adds *in his lifetime.*

Then she adds his list of accomplishments. She now has:

Barack Obama has accomplished a lot in his lifetime. He was a senator. He is an author. He is President, and he won the Nobel Peace Prize.

I suggest to Isabella, "You might want to add *of the United States* after you say he is President."

Isabella makes some changes and then says, "I should also add he is the first black President."

"Great idea. I know you mentioned it before in your paper, but now you are restating the most important things. That is what some writers do when they write their conclusions."

Isabella's reads her conclusion so far:

Barack Obama has accomplished a lot in his lifetime. He was a lawyer and a senator. He is an author. He is the first black President of the United States, and he won the Nobel Peace Prize.

"I love this conclusion. I think it needs one more sentence though. Maybe you can ask a question or make a bold statement. A lot of students are writing about people who have died, but President Obama is still alive. Do you think he will achieve any other things? Does he inspire you?"

Isabella adds: *He is an inspiration to people all over the world.*

"Wow! Great thinking. That is the perfect ending sentence. Well done!"

Students Make Final Revisions

When students finish drafting and revising, they work with peers to make their final revisions and edits. They read to each other, and I encourage students to listen with a critical ear, adding "Feel free to give advice and ask questions if something doesn't make sense. Make sure you help correct any spelling, capitals, or punctuation errors." I have each peer editor sign the bottom of his or her partner's draft, which ensures they take their peer editor job seriously.

I circle around the room and take notes, recording what I see and hear from students. I focus on these questions: *Are the peers really listening? Are they making suggestions and asking questions? Do they seem to really be checking for spelling, punctuation, and capitalization errors to the best of their abilities?*

After this session, I gather students and review what I saw and heard. I share specific questions and comments I heard. Then I ask volunteers to share how their peers helped them with an idea or an edit. We talk about the importance of having peer editors, especially when we are working on big projects.

> ### Teaching Tip
> Using peers to help revise and edit is an excellent way to teach the importance of rereading and examining one's writing.

Students Publish

Now that the tough work is finished, students type their papers. We have many options for this. We have a computer lab, and we have a few computers in my classroom. Students can also type at home, with family members there to help.

A fun option after this research paper is finished is to actually "make" the famous person from paper, paints, markers, and other materials. Students look forward to this part of the project. They love seeing all the people of history hanging in our room as we share our reports over the next couple of weeks.

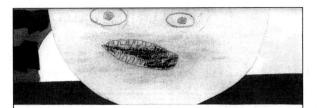

Davy Crockett

by Irvin

Davy Crockett was an interesting person. He was born in Tennessee on August 17th, 1788. When Davy was a child, he learned to hunt and fish. When he was twelve years old, he went on a cattle drive to get money. He went three hundred miles and he did not know how to get home. He met some travelers who helped him get home. Davy did not like school. He got in fight with a boy. He thought he would get in trouble from his dad so he ran away and went on another cattle drive. He took other jobs and after two years, Davy came home.

Davy was friendly and funny. He said funny things. As Davy grew older he worked for a farmer. He was good at shooting a rifle. He hunted animals like bears and deer. Davy married Polly Finley in 1806. He joined the Army in 1813. He fought the Indians. Davy was elected to the Tennessee legislature and elected to the U.S. Congress in 1828. Davy was poor and uneducated. He still became a Congressman. He wanted to help the Americans settling in Texas to be free from Mexican rule. Davy defended The Alamo.

Davy got married again and had four children. His new wife's name was Elizabeth Patton. Davy called himself, "half horse, half alligator with a touch of snapping turtle." His famous saying was, "Be sure you're right. Then go ahead." Davy died defending The Alamo March 6, 1836. Davy helped others and fought for what he believed in.

Harriet Tubman

by Alex

Harriet Tubman was an amazing woman. She was born in 1821 in Maryland. Both her parents, Ben and Harriet Ross, were slaves. As a child, she was called Minty. Minty loved playing with her brothers and sisters. When she turned six, she was sold to work for Mrs. Cook. There, she had to wind yarn and help Mr. Cook catch muskrats. Minty couldn't do the job and was sold to Miss Susan. She was then sent outside to do field work. One day Minty helped a slave escape but was hit on the forehead by a two-pound weight. The wound left a scar on her forehead but many people treated her with respect. From then on, she was called Harriet.

When she was about twenty-three, Harriet married John Tubman. Dreaming of freedom, Harriet left John and traveled up north. She became a passenger on the Underground Railroad. She reached Pennsylvania and became a free woman. Wanting to share her freedom with her family, she promised to go back to get them. Along the way, she became the conductor of the Underground Railroad. She helped her family and hundreds of other people escape to freedom.

When the Civil War started, Harriet worked as a nurse and a spy for the Union Army. Once the Civil War was over, Harriet returned home to help her parents. Seeing that other former slaves needed help, she opened her home to them. She earned money by giving speeches. She once said, "I was the conductor of the Underground Railroad for eight years, and can say what most conductors can't say. I never ran my train off the track and I never lost a passenger." In 1913 Harriet Tubman caught pneumonia and died at the age of 92 in Auburn, New York. Harriet will always be remembered for her devotion to people.

FIGURE 10.8 *Final student research reports*

✳ Final Thoughts

There are many options for research reports. We used three sources for ours. If you have third graders, maybe one or two sources would be enough. There are also many kinds of graphic organizers that work for note-taking. Find one that works for your students, or create your own. Maybe it looks a lot like the one we used. Maybe it is different.

Remember, too, that there are different formats for publishing research reports as well. One of my favorites comes from a colleague. She used a *Time for Kids* format for reporting on a famous person. Be creative. Sometimes the format is an element that encourages students to be excited about a research report.

· · · · · · · · ·

This book started out as a reply to a group of teachers who asked me to write lessons for teaching what was most important in writing. Some years have passed and now we have the Common Core State Standards. I am thrilled that writing has taken an equal place among the subjects in our standards. My hope with this book is that, rather than being overwhelmed by the new standards, these lessons will support you one step at a time as you work to teach your students to write different text types and more specific genres. I used an old tried and true formula:

1. Let students explore.

2. Use mentor texts.

3. Model writing.

4. Engage students in shared writing.

5. Guide students to write independently. (This includes one-to-one conferences and small group teaching for those who are having trouble.)

I hope you will take these lessons, tweak them, make them your own, and explore further lessons to teach and extend learning in the area of writing.

Name _____ Date _____

Planning Graphic Organizer: Narrative/Memoir

Introduction: Where/When/Who/What

Event 1

Event 2

Event 3

Conclusion: Why is this story important to you? How does it affect your life now?

Name _____ Date _____

Assessment Checklist

	YES	NO
I have a title.	_____	_____
I have a lead sentence.	_____	_____
I elaborated with details.	_____	_____
I used interesting words.	_____	_____

They are _____

_____

	YES	NO
I have an ending sentence.	_____	_____
I have at least two paragraphs with two main ideas.	_____	_____

My first paragraph is about _____.

My second paragraph is about _____.

	YES	NO
I indented my paragraphs and checked for spelling and capital letters.	_____	_____

10 Essential Writing Lessons © 2013 by Megan Sloan, Scholastic Teaching Resources

Name _____ Date _____

Character _____

Character Traits With Evidence Organizer

Character Trait Adjective used to describe	Evidence From the Text What does this character say, do, or think? What do others say about him/her?

Name _____ Date _____

Literary Essay Graphic Organizer: Character

Lead: Introduce the character and book.

Body or Middle: Give background about the character and story. Discuss two character traits and
provide evidence.

Conclusion: Why is the character strong and unforgettable? How did he or she change and/or affect
other people?

10 Essential Writing Lessons © 2013 by Megan Sloan, Scholastic Teaching Resources

Name _____ Date _____

Planning Graphic Organizer: Informative Article

Introduction: Get the readers' attention.

Topic 1

Topic 2

Topic 3

Conclusion: Restate the most important idea from the introduction.

Name _____ Date _____

Planning Graphic Organizer: Opinion Piece

Opening Paragraph: Introduce topic and state opinion.

Reason or Fact to Support:

Reason or Fact to Support:

Reason or Fact to Support:

Conclusion: Restate opinion. Maybe suggest what can be done and why.

10 Essential Writing Lessons © 2013 by Megan Sloan, Scholastic Teaching Resources

Name _____ Date _____

Research Note-Taking Sheet

	Question:
Source 1	Notes:
Source 2	Notes:
Source 3	Notes:

Name _____ Date _____

Topic _____ Paragraph _____

Drafting Sheet

Opening Sentence _____

_____

_____

Complete Paragraph: Include at least 7–10 interesting facts from your notes. Attach notebook paper if you need more space.

_____

_____

_____

_____

_____

_____

_____

_____

_____

_____

_____

_____

 10 Essential Writing Lessons © 2013 by Megan Sloan, Scholastic Teaching Resources

References

Professional Books

Common Core State Standards Initiative (2010). *Common Core State Standards for English Language Arts*.

Fox, M. (1993). *Radical reflections: Passionate opinions on teaching, learning, and living*. San Diego: Harcourt.

Graves, D. (1994). *A fresh look at writing*. Portsmouth, NH: Heinemann.

Routman, R. (2005). *Writing essentials*. Portsmouth, NH: Heinemann.

Children's Books

Aller, S. (2004). *Sitting Bull*. New York: Barnes and Noble.

Adler, D. (1990). *A picture book of Helen Keller*. New York: Holiday House.

Applegate, K. (2012). *The one and only Ivan*. New York: HarperCollins.

Avi. (1995). *Poppy*. New York: HarperCollins.

_____. (1990). *The true confessions of Charlotte Doyle*. New York: Orchard.

Berne, E. (2009). *Helen Keller: Courage in darkness*. New York: Sterling.

Bishop, N. (2008). *Frogs*. New York: Scholastic.

Bruel, N. (2006). *Who is Melvin Bubble?* New Milford, CT: Roaring Book Press.

Bunting, E. (1995). *Once upon a time (Meet the author)*. Katonah, NY: Richard C. Owen.

_____. (1993). *Someday a tree*. New York: Clarion.

_____. (1999). *Smoky night*. Orlando, FL: Harcourt.

_____. (1992). *The wall*. New York: Clarion.

Cooney, B. (1996). *Eleanor*. New York: Viking Press.

_____. (1982). *Miss Rumphius*. New York: Viking Penguin.

Coles, R. (1995). *The story of Ruby Bridges*. New York: Scholastic.

Crews, D. (1991). *Big mama's*. New York: Greenwillow.

_____. (1996). *Shortcut*. New York: Greenwillow.

Dahl, R. (2011). *James and the giant peach*. New York: Penguin Classics.

Dennis, B., Nethery, M., & Larson, K. (2009). *Nubs: The true story of a mutt, a marine, and a miracle*. Boston: Little Brown.

DePalma, M.N. (2005). *A grand old tree*. New York: Scholastic.

DiCamillo, K. (2000). *Because of Winn-Dixie*. Cambridge, MA: Candlewick Press.

_____. *Tale of Despereaux*. Cambridge, MA: Candlewick Press.

Dotlich, R.K. (1998). *Lemonade sun and other summer poems*. Honesdale, PA: Wordsong/Boyds Mills Press.

Editors of *Time for Kids*. (2005). *Harriet Tubman: A woman of courage*. New York: HarperCollins.

Fleming, D. (1996). *Where once there was a wood*. New York: Henry Holt.

_____. (2003). *Maker of things (Meet the author)*. Katonah, NY: Richard C. Owen.

Fletcher, R. (2000). *A writing kind of day: Poems for young poets*. Honesdale, PA: Boyds Mills Press.

Florian, D. (2006). *Handsprings*. New York: Greenwillow.

_____. (1998). *Insectlopedia*. Orlando: Harcourt.

_____. (2005). *See for yourself (Meet the author)*. Katona, NY: Richard C. Owen.

_____. (1999). *Winter eyes*. New York: Greenwillow.

Gagne, P.R., & Kerruish, S. (Producers). (2000). *Miss Rumphius* [video]. USA: Westwood Studios, Inc. and Spellbound Production, Inc. (Available through Safari Montage, https://www.safarimontage.com)

Gardiner, J.R. (1980). *Stone fox*. New York: HarperCollins.

George, J.C. (1995). *There's an owl in the shower*. New York: HarperCollins.

Gibbons, G. (2000). *My baseball book*. Singapore: Tien Wah Press.

_____. (1994). *Emergency*. New York: Holiday House.

_____. (1999). *Penguins*. New York: Holiday House.

_____. (1992). *Recycle!* Boston: Little, Brown & Company.

_____. (1995). *Wolves*. New York: Holiday House.

Graff, S. (1965). *Helen Keller*. New York: Bantam Doubleday Dell.

Graves, D. (1996). *Baseball, snakes and summer squash: poems about growing up*. Honesdale, PA: Boyds Mills Press

Greenfield, E. (1978). *Honey, I love and other love poems*. New York: Harper & Row.

Greenfield, E. (1988). *Under the Sunday tree*. New York: HarperCollins.

Gutman, Dan. (1997). *Honus and me*. New York: Avon.

Hopkins, L.B. (1993). *Extra innings: Baseball poems*. San Diego: Harcourt.

_____. (1991). *Good books, good times!* New York: HarperCollins.

_____. (2011). *I am the book*. New York: Holiday House.

_____. (2010). *Sharing the seasons: A book of poems*. New York: Simon & Schuster.

Houston, G. (1992). *My Great-Aunt Arizona*. New York: HarperCollins.

Howker, J. (1997). *Walk with a wolf*. Cambridge, MA: Candlewick Press.

Johnston, T. (1994). *Amber on the mountain*. New York: Penguin.

Kallaher, K. (2011). *Team time*. Scholastic News, Edition 3, September 5, 2011.

Laminack, L.L. (2004). *Saturdays and teacakes*. Atlanta: Peachtree Publisher.

Levenson, G. (1999). *Pumpkin circle: The story of a garden*. Berkeley, CA: Tricycle Press.

Levine, E. (2007). *Henry's freedom box: A true story from the underground railroad.* New York: Scholastic

Lewis, J.P. (1998). *Doodle dandies: Poems that take shape.* New York: Simon & Schuster.

Lobel, A. (1980). *Fables.* New York: Scholastic.

London, J. (1996). *The eyes of gray wolf.* San Francisco: Chronicle.

Lundell, M. & Trivas, I. (1995). *A girl named Helen Keller.* New York: Scholastic.

MacLachlan, P. (1994). *All the places to love.* New York: HarperCollins.

MacLachlan, P & MacLachlan Charest, E. (2006). *Once I ate a pie.* New York: HarperCollins.

Mannis, C.D. (2002). *One leaf rides the wind.* New York: Penguin.

Mansfield, Massachusetts, St. Mary's Catholic School. (2005). *Haiku hike.* New York: Scholastic.

Masoff, J. (2002). *Everest: Reaching for the sky.* New York: Scholastic.

Mathers, P. (1991). *Sophie and Lou.* New York: Simon & Schuster.

McCloskey, R. (1957). *Time of wonder.* New York: Viking.

McDonough, Y.Z. (2005). *Who was Louis Armstrong?* New York: Penguin Young Readers.

Modigliani, L. (2012). School on a bus. *Scholastic News,* Edition 4, March 19, 2012.

Noe, K. S. (2011). *Something to hold.* New York: Clarion.

Obama, B. (2010). *Of thee I sing: A letter to my daughters.* New York: Knopf.

O'Brien, R.C. (1971). *Mrs. Frisby and the rats of NIMH.* New York: Simon & Schuster.

Paolilli, P. & Brewer, P. (2001). *Silver Seeds: A book of nature poems.* New York: Viking Press.

Paulson, G. (1987). *Hatchet.* New York: Simon & Schuster.

Parton, D.. (1994). *Coat of many colors.* New York: HarperCollins.

Pinkney, A. (1998). *Duke Ellington.* New York: Hyperion.

Polacco, P. (2001). *Betty doll.* New York: Philomel.

_____. (1995). *My ol' man.* New York: Philomel Books.

_____. (1998). *Thank you, Mr. Falker.* New York: Philomel.

_____. (1990). *Thundercake.* New York: Putnam & Grosset.

Ransom, C. (2005). *Daniel Boone.* Minneapolis, MN: Lerner Publications.

Ringgold, F. (1992). *Aunt Harriet's underground railroad in the sky.* New York: Crown.

Ryan, P. M. (2001). *Hello ocean.* Watertown, MA: Talewinds.

Rylant, C. (2000). *In November.* San Diego: Harcourt.

_____. (1985). *The relatives came.* New York: Scholastic.

_____. (1982). *When I was young in the mountains.* New York: Penguin.

Sachar, L. (1998). *Holes.* New York: Farrar, Straus & Girroux.

Sams, C.R. II. & Jean Stoick. (2007). *First snow in the woods.* Altona, Manitoba: Friesens.

Scholastic News Staff. (2012). Blast from the past. *Scholastic News, Edition 3*, January 2, 2012.

_____. (2011). Rough road ahead. *Scholastic News, Edition 3*, March 21, 2011.

Sidman, J. (1985). *Dark emperor and other poems of the night.* New York: Houghton Mifflin.

_____. (2007). *This is just to say: Poems of apology and forgiveness.* New York: Houghton Mifflin.

Thompson, G. (2003). *Who was Helen Keller?* New York: Grosset & Dunlap.

Time for Kids Staff (2011). Dino feathers. *Time for Kids, Edition 3-4*, September 30, 2011.

_____. (2011). Next stop: Mars. *Time for Kids, Edition 5-6*, November 11, 2011.

White, E.B. (1952). *Charlotte's web.* New York: Harper & Row.

Wild, M. (2006). *Fox.* La Jolla, CA: Kane/Miller.

Wiles, D. (2005). *Each little bird that sings.* Orlando: Harcourt.

_____. 2001. *Love, Ruby Lavender.* Orlando: Harcourt.

Winget, M. (2003). *Eleanor Roosevelt.* New York: Barnes & Noble.

Winter, J. (2005). *The Librarian of Basra: A true story from Iraq.* Orlando, FL.: Harcourt.

_____. (1998). *My name is Georgia.* Orlando: Harcourt.

_____. (2007). *The tale of pale male: A true story.* Orlando: Harcourt.

_____. (2008). *Wangari's trees of peace: A true story from Africa.* Orlando: Harcourt.

Wong, J. (2006). *Before it wriggles away.* Katonah, NY: Richard C. Owen.

Worth, V. (1994). *All the small poems and fourteen more.* New York: Farrar, Straus & Giroux.

Yolen, J. (2003). *Color me a rhyme: Nature poems for young people.* Honesdale, PA: Boyds Mills Press.

_____. (2007). *Shape me a rhyme: Nature's forms in poetry.* Honesdale, PA: Boyds Mills Press.

_____. (1987). *Owl moon.* New York: Philomel.

Adult Literature

Walls, Jeanette. (2009). *Half Broke Horses.* New York: Scribner.

Magazines

Kids Discover

National Geographic for Kids

Scholastic News

Sports Illustrated for Kids

Time for Kids

Zoobooks

Online Resources

Scholastic Printables: *More Miracles for Helen Keller: An Unexpected Hero*

New World Encyclopedia Online